NO NONSENSE

ATTRACT
New Customers

NO NONSENSE

ATTRACT
New Customers

100+ Ideas to Bring In
More Customers

Jerry R. Wilson

This edition first published in 2020 by Career Press, an imprint of
Red Wheel/Weiser, LLC
With offices at:
65 Parker Street, Suite 7
Newburyport, MA 01950
www.careerpress.com
www.redwheelweiser.com

ISBN: 978-1-63265-180-8
Library of Congress Cataloging-in-Publication Data available upon request.

Cover Design by Kathryn Sky-Peck
Interior by Steve Amarillo / Urban Design LLC
Typeset in Adobe Dapifer and Minion Pro

Printed in the United States of America
IBI
10 9 8 7 6 5 4 3 2 1

Contents

How to Use This Book

Every quick idea in this book has been selected to help you—directly or indirectly—gain and retain customers, create relationships, and build a successful business.

Don't try to implement all these ideas at once, because some may not be a good fit right now. Read through them all and select only those that can really make a difference at the moment. Don't worry, you can go back and review the others periodically.

Place your ideas into three categories:

1. Those to implement now.

2. Those to review again in thirty days.

3. Those to pass along to an associate.

Involve your staff in selecting and implementing these ideas, and don't forget to give credit for their success! Invest in additional copies of this book and distribute them among your staff. Get everyone involved in selecting and recommending various quick ideas.

Revisit this book every ninety days. As your business changes, you will find new quick ideas that may suit you better now that competition is heating up.

Remember, all the ideas in this book have been proven in businesses across the United States and around the world. They have worked for others and will work for you!

One Thing Worse Than a Rude Employee

Not every person is cut out to help you prospect for new customers. You've been told before and you'll hear it again: Hire for attitude; train for aptitude. The people in your business who meet and greet customers have to do it with a smile. Prospecting for customers requires people with a pleasing, positive, and agreeable attitude. Anyone without that mindset needs to leave your business!

ACTION ITEM

If you have people who are not willing to work to bring in new customers, evaluate whether they should stay in your business. Good prospectors evaluate the people who are helping them achieve their goals.

When an Illinois farm-implement dealership confronted the fact that their parts manager was a walking encyclopedia on tractors, combines, and implement equipment, they also had to admit he was the most cantankerous guy east of the Rocky Mountains. He constantly aggravated fellow employees and drove away customers. They finally reached a decision and invited him to pursue other employment. Immediately after this problem employee left, many prospects returned to the company and became customers. It seems that he had alienated a great number of people over the years who had decided to avoid the dealership. Once he was gone, however, things changed, and business soon picked up.

TAKEAWAY

The only thing worse than allowing rogue employees to destroy your attempts to get new customers is paying them to do it!

WAY 2

Bribe Significant Others

There's nothing better than selling prospects, but it doesn't hurt to include their spouses or significant others in your sales efforts. In fact, a significant other may become the key motivator to get your prospect to become your customer. After all, it's always helpful to have more influence with your prospects.

ACTION ITEM

Start now to build a database of your prospects' and customers' partners, family names, and home addresses. In the days and years to come, this list will be as valuable as any you will ever have.

When a major distributor was planning his sales conference at the Opryland Hotel in Nashville, TN, he decided to invite his prospects' significant others. His company had worked hard to build a database with all their names. He sent a special message to their homes offering an all-expenses-paid weekend at the conference, complete with hors d'oeuvres, good food, a touch of business, and some classy entertainment. Throw in a really deluxe room, a bottle of wine, a gift card to pay for incidentals, and some free time to enjoy Opryland, and the entire event became a huge success. It's even conceivable that some of the spouses and significant others may have been more sold on the company than the original prospects were! Regardless, the event paid off in a big way, and the major distributor earned some major new customers.

Involve the Family

If you truly want to build long-term name recognition and convince prospects that you are the best choice, mailing to their homes can have a huge payoff. Obviously, you need to be careful what you send and make sure it's appropriate to tell and sell your story, but your creative choices are endless. Use cartoons, fun newsletters, or contests to involve the family.

ACTION ITEM

Think about what you can do to involve your prospects' and customers' families. It's a great way, at little or no expense, to tell and sell your story and convert those hard-headed prospects into big-buying customers. Let their families help you convince them to join you.

When a Virginia-based tire company wanted to involve both its employees and its prospects in understanding more about what the company was doing to grow, be successful, and serve its customers, it began mailing a high-quality newsletter to the homes of all prospects and customers in its database. The newsletter contained a code number. Each month, they randomly called two homes. If the person who answered the phone had read the newsletter and could recite the number, the company immediately sent two crisp, clean $100 bills. That amounted to $400 each month. But in the process, the company convinced about 1,000 prospects and customers to know about their newsletter, look forward to its arrival, and be involved in the information it provided.

TAKEAWAY

You can't have too much help when it comes to convincing prospects to be your customers. Don't be shy about reaching out to families—it's a win-win situation for everyone involved.

WAY 4

Prospect with a T-E-A-M

Prospecting should be a team effort in your company. The acronym T-E-A-M stands for Together Everyone Accomplishes More. There's something about the energy, synergy, excitement, enthusiasm, and creativity of a group of people working together to win customers that can't be achieved in any other way. For this quick idea, our recommendation is that you form a team and call it your prospecting task force.

ACTION ITEM

Form a prospecting task force today, then follow these ideas and watch what happens. Make sure you pick a diverse group of people, and don't be afraid to move people in and out as you discover how the team works together.

Each Tuesday morning at 7:00 a.m., a group of people from different departments gathers at a restaurant to do their prospect planning for the week. The coordinator, their national sales manager, starts the meeting by reviewing their top ten prospects from the previous week and the results from the action plan they put together the previous Tuesday. Following that, they create a new Top 10 agenda. After that list of ten is in place, they brainstorm a few action items for the week and assign various task-force members to follow through. Their real secret is the energy and synergy that flows out of the group. An excellent example of this comes from Ray Kroc, the founder of McDonald's, who said: "No one of us is as smart as all of us."

TAKEAWAY

Don't wait for something to happen. If you get your task force together today, you can make it happen!

Use Your People

Why do you need to get new customers? Is it because your business is poorly run and you keep losing the ones you have? Are you ready to fill the capacity of your plant or establish a new location? Do you want to get more volume for economies of scale or replace the natural attrition that all businesses experience?

Hopefully, it's because you want your business to grow.

If growth is your objective, remember what a huge opportunity educating prospects and customers can produce for you. One of my favorite quotes is: "Your business must grow for people to grow, and people must grow for your business to grow." Think about how the explosion of technology can help you make education a cornerstone of your prospecting efforts. As William Arthur Ward said: "The mediocre teacher tells, the good teacher explains, the superior teacher demonstrates, and the great teacher inspires." Remember those words when developing your own educational program. Smart associates make smart decisions, which can help you develop a better business.

ACTION ITEM

Examine your sales team and workforce. Evaluate their skills and explore educational or training opportunities to increase their skills. Then examine current technologies that can be harnessed to help you sell and create relationships with customers.

Examine the finances of any major university and you will find that its alumni are the driving force behind its success. Universities harness the power of their former students and their educations.

> **TAKEAWAY**
>
> *Never overlook the power of education for your employees if you want to enhance your business.*

WAY 6

Call Them Associates

One of the awkward things many business owners must decide is what to call their coworkers. Should they be labeled "employees," "staff," "crew," "the workforce," or some other descriptive term? My choice, after careful research, is to call them *associates*. If you practice servant-leadership—a style of leadership that endeavors to serve others, rather than focusing on power or trying to take control—then you believe that your goal is to create relationships with potential customers. You and your workers are associating together to serve and to help, which makes for a beneficial relationship.

ACTION ITEM

Address and treat your employees as associates, with respect and dignity. If you do this, they'll soon see themselves as, and start acting like, true associates. But this idea can backfire if your employees don't really see themselves as associates.

Sam Walton's wife convinced him to use the term "associates" when the Wal-Mart empire was in its early days and they were just starting to be successful, both in growth and market share. She believed that, by sharing the bounty, their people would perform and embrace the complete Wal-Mart idea. Did it work? If you've ever been in a Wal-Mart store early in the morning when employees have their store meeting and do the Wal-Mart cheer, you know that these associates truly believe in the values and benefits that their company promotes. Many Wal-Mart associates have since become stockholders and gone on to become quite wealthy.

If You Want Loyalty

Whether you work with one, two, ten, or 100 other people who can help you get new customers, there will be times when it's important to show them your appreciation in a tangible way. It may be as simple as bringing in some doughnuts for everyone or as important as holding an annual dinner to show your coworkers and associates how much you appreciate their help. Whatever their form, think about giving tangible rewards. You might even consider sharing some of that reward money!

ACTION ITEM

Thank your employees in a tangible way for the help they've given you, and they'll be quick to help you again tomorrow. Your people are looking for more than just a pat on the back and a thank you.

When Cindy's boss saw a pile of new correspondence on his desk, he knew that Cindy had been hard at work. On top of the pile was a note that said: "If you want loyalty, get a dog. I work for money." In addition to making him smile, this got her boss wondering if she were sending him a message. When he asked her about it, Cindy laughed and said: "No, I wasn't asking for a raise, although I do work for money. I simply thought you would see it as fun, and enjoy it." While he enjoyed it, it also made an impression on him. He realized that sometimes it's important to do more than just say "thank you." Employees always appreciate tangible rewards, and loyalty can be rewarded in many different ways.

TAKEAWAY

What gets rewarded, gets repeated.

Make Me Feel Important

Think back to the last time you had that really warm glow inside when somebody made you feel special—perhaps because they saw a sign hanging around your neck that said M-M-F-I (Make Me Feel Important)! One of the basic principles of winning customers away from your competition is to make them feel wanted, needed, and appreciated. Every time you see prospects or customers, mentally hang that sign around their necks and do something to make them feel important.

ACTION ITEM

Brainstorm what you can do to make people feel important. Develop a system to do it every day and with every customer.

Gayle is a regional vice president for a major insurance company. She has grasped the M-M-F-I principle and turned it into one of her tools to gain and retain customers. When she's attempting to get prospects to represent her company in a particular area, or when she wants to get existing customers to do something special to benefit her other customers, one of her techniques is to put them on a pedestal by reminding them that they are the best of the best. When she asks them to do something, she makes it clear that she only selects the most outstanding people. Rarely does anyone say "no," and those who do work with her often develop into loyal customers. Gayle has been able to convert many skeptical prospects into delighted customers by understanding their needs and making them feel important.

WAY 9

Strategic Partnerships

Most companies talk about building a relationship with their prospects as they turn them into customers. Unfortunately, many companies often exploit those relationships, taking as much as they can get and even making sales that their customers don't need. Try to be different and see your prospects as a true partners. You should work together to be more profitable and productive.

ACTION ITEM

List your customers and prospects. Then identify why you have a good relationship with each one or why you don't. Work to strengthen these relationships until you've created a true marriage of equals.

Mike, a silver-haired and highly successful business owner, left prospecting to his sales force. They had the job to wine and dine prospects until they believed a personal visit from the owner and boss might convince someone to come aboard as a customer. When Mike arrived at the prospect's place of business, he placed a nondescript brown box on the table in the conference room where the meeting was to take place. When prospects asked what was in the box—as they always did—he removed the lid to reveal a cake, forks, knives, and plates. He told them that his intention was that they form a partnership that day and celebrate it by cutting the cake—kind of like a quasi-marriage. This strategy was a huge success and, in almost every case, the cake and Mike's presence pushed prospects over the edge. Mike created and maintained a true partnership with all of his customers.

WAY 10

Play It S-A-F-E

Let's face it—prospecting is hard work, time-consuming, and expensive. But it's a necessary evil. Regardless of your feelings about cold-calling, prospecting, and constantly looking for new customers, it has to be done. You don't have to like it, but you have to do it. The key is to make your prospects feel S-A-F-E (Secure, Accepted, Free of Fear, and Enthusiastic) in the process.

ACTION ITEM

Always follow the acronym S-A-F-E (Secure, Accepted, Free of Fear, and Enthusiastic) to make sure that people know it's okay to come to your events. Feeling safe is an incredibly important part of any relationship.

One local ministry director invited about ninety church pastors to join him for a free lunch. He presented a no-pressure, no-selling, no-embarrassment agenda on how his ministry could help them grow their churches. It was promoted by a series of three mailings, an email, and a telephone campaign. How many people can pass up a free lunch?

After the luncheon, this savvy director encouraged the entire audience to fill out a questionnaire about how they could use his services. He immediately called on those who indicated interest in one or more of his services and worked to build a relationship with them. For those who didn't indicate any interest, he had at least met them in person so he could start working to build personal relationships that could eventually turn them into mission supporters.

> **TAKEAWAY**
> ---
> *The best way to reduce your cost of prospecting and get results is to host a breakfast or lunch during business hours. Pair up a sizzling agenda with a free meal, and you'll be surprised at how quickly your prospects become loyal customers.*

People-to-People Prospecting

One quick idea to encourage prospects is to assign an inside person as their direct contact. Then train those insiders to know a lot about the prospects and to be ready if they call. It gives each prospect a name and a face with which to connect and can be tremendously encouraging in getting them to make that first call to your company.

ACTION ITEM

Use vendors who work with digital photography to produce affordable and classy business cards that can be updated and kept fresh at little or no cost. There are many sources for photo business cards and, with today's technology, you can have them made up faster than ever.

One large car dealership, upon learning about this idea, made a dramatic change in how they approached their prospects and customers when they realized they were actually trying to sell people not cars. They began using business cards with associates' pictures printed on them. On the back of the cards were brief stories about the associates, their history with the company, and their commitment to customers. They also printed an 8 1/2" ×

11" page with pictures of all their inside customer-service people along with their names, titles, and extension numbers. Now, when customers call that dealership, they know more about the people with whom they're dealing. It has been very successful for them, and it will be for you as well.

WAY 12

Birds of a Feather

One of the most valuable, stimulating, creative, and exciting things you can do is to network with other businesses who operate as you do but who aren't your direct competitors. Even better, make opportunities to visit other facilities similar to yours to see what different companies are using as business models. This helps both parties learn from their mutual strengths and weaknesses and lets them benefit from each others' successes and failures.

ACTION ITEM

Consider putting together your own small group to identify other companies like yours and build relationships that can pay off for everyone involved. There are many resources that can help you identify these companies. The secret is to understand that help is out there!

A medical clinic in the Northeast had an unbelievable track record for attracting patients. They had successfully used their system and infrastructure for almost twenty years, but they realized that new ideas similar to theirs could have a huge payoff. Through a medical association, they were able to identify a dozen other clinics across the United States very similar to theirs, but in noncompetitive locations. They sent a broadcast letter to these clinics and quickly formed a small group that meets twice a year. They spend two days together reviewing their facilities, talking about their operations, and generally brainstorming about what is working and what is not for each of them. It's amazing how, when a group of businesspeople come together to share their very best ideas, everyone goes home with new excitement for their business. It's probably one of the biggest payoffs that you can get if you are working on a serious and ongoing prospecting effort.

WAY 13

Get Them on Your Own Turf

In developing new customers, it's important to understand how power influences your efforts to convince prospects to do business with you. Any time you're in your customers' place of business or on their turf, you're at a major disadvantage. They have the power and the control to guide and direct what happens. A better idea is to get them on neutral turf, where you can interact as equals. The ideal situation is to get them on *your* turf, where you can direct the action and capture their complete attention.

ACTION ITEM

Discuss techniques to get prospective customers away from their offices and onto neutral turf. Then explore ideas that can bring prospects onto your turf, where you are in the power position.

Dave is a master at forging relationships with new customers. One of his strategies is to do everything he can to get prospects onto neutral territory. When Dave has a special offer or a tantalizing deal, he invites prospects to join him for breakfast, coffee, lunch, or an afternoon break so he can have their total attention. When he can, he tries to get them to visit him at his office. This puts Dave in the power position. What are you doing to get your prospects on neutral territory so you can have an even chance to get them as new customers?

> **TAKEAWAY**
>
> *When you're ready to make a great presentation, invite prospects to meet you for a meal or coffee to get them out of their familiar environments and into your sphere of influence.*

Become a Joiner

All trades, professions, and occupations have associations that you can join. These trade and professional groups can be a tremendous resource to help you keep up with changes, network with the most successful people in your specialty, and see how other people operate. There are two key secrets to being part of an association—look at the dues as an investment instead of as a cost, and remember that you have to get involved to get value. To get value out of being a joiner, remember the acronym R-A-V-E—Read all the materials, Attend the events, Volunteer on projects, and Enjoy the social outlet.

ACTION ITEM

Look around to see what local, regional, or national associations can be of benefit to you. Handpick a few that you want to explore and contact them about becoming an active member. Remember to R-A-V-E (Read, Attend, Volunteer, Enjoy)!

Mae struggled with how to pay employees when some came to work and some didn't during a horrendous snowstorm. She struggled with it until it was time to go to an association meeting. Upon arriving, she found that everyone in her position had agonized over the same problem. She was not alone. When she left the meeting that day, she had answers, as well as a list of people she could call when she faced similar indecision in the future. There's nothing better to help you learn more than active membership in a good association.

WAY 15

Intentional Relationships

Have you ever wondered how often chance or coincidence has guided you into an important relationship? If you have a spouse, a best friend, or a significant other in your life, it is likely that you met by coincidence. But after that first meeting, you made time to build on the relationship. It became an *intentional* relationship because you created the time and space to get to know each other. The main thing to grasp from this quick idea is the word "intentional," because it means you made an effort and invested in the relationship. Hopefully, all your intentional relationships will be quality investments that pay off.

ACTION ITEM

Make "intentional" part of your vocabulary to describe the relationships you want to have—now and in the future.

One of the reasons we talk about giving exceptional service throughout this book is because it is the means by which to create positive relationships. When you concentrate on building intentional relationships, you create business, which translates into increased profits for you. But before you can do that, you have to do the things you promise and demonstrate outstanding service. That's how you turn prospects into customers—by developing intentional relationships.

> **TAKEAWAY**
>
> *Chance can open many doors, but you can only walk through them with the right intentions. Intentional relationships take time and effort, but they are definitely worth it!*

Are You New or Recycled?

New customers want to be fussed over. They want to feel special. They want to be recognized, accepted, and appreciated for bringing their business to you. But new customers are not more important than old customers, and it's important to remember to appreciate them both. What you need is a system that recognizes recycled customers who have returned and identifies and rewards new people who have come aboard for the first time. The key is to make that happen every day with every customer.

ACTION ITEM

Set up a database to identify and track new and returning customers. Then devise a simple yet effective method that consistently rewards both.

A group of California bowling alleys developed a system to reward both returning customers and prospects who were coming in for the first time. They asked a simple question: "Have you bowled with us before?" If customers said "yes," a manager stopped by while they were bowling and thanked them for coming in again. He also gave them a few coupons good for their next visit. If customers said they were there for the first time, they were handed a simple brochure that identified a few key things that made that bowling alley different. The manager also stopped by and thanked them for coming in, giving them a coupon for free beverages and another good for their next visit. What are you doing to identify your new customers, while still rewarding the old?

> **TAKEAWAY**
>
> *Everyone wants to feel special, so make sure your customers know how much they mean to you. Customers will go where they feel invited and return to where they feel appreciated.*

WAY 17

Love That Loyalty

Part of searching for new customers is occasionally encountering those who hold you at arm's length because of their loyalty to their current suppliers. Inevitably, they will tell you stories about how their current vendors have gone the extra mile for them. Our instinct, when attempting to get business, is to be defensive and try to overcome that loyalty. That's exactly the wrong thing to do.

It only alienates prospects and makes it unlikely that you will ever get their business. There is a better way to approach the situation.

ACTION ITEM

Value loyalty, and tell your prospects you do. Then keep right on pitching. At some point, their needs will change or their current suppliers will fail them. You want to be there for them when that happens.

When people describe their loyalty, first compliment them. If you really think about it, loyalty is a good character trait. Wouldn't you like all of your customers to be so loyal that they throw all your competition out the door? Second, acknowledge that loyalty is a rare commodity that is all too often missing in business today. At least that's the commonly held perception, although I believe there are more loyal people out there than we recognize.

> **TAKEAWAY**
>
> *Remember, loyalty comes from customer delight. Make sure you are ready to catch prospects when they fall, and you'll have new customers who are loyal to you.*

Develop a Clear Vision of Success

Psychologists, motivational experts, and various authors have posited that you can become the vision that you have of yourself in your mind. This technique, called "visualizing," is a tool that can help you achieve great success.

ACTION ITEM

Create a vision for your company and write it down. Create posters, brief everyone in the company, put it on your answering machine or voice mail, and tag it to your letterhead. Surround yourself with your vision of success.

James Allen, highly respected author of *As a Man Thinketh*, says that our mission is to develop pictures in our minds that will lead us to success. For example, picture your prospects as your customers. Picture them in your mind joining you for strategy sessions and filling out big orders. Picture them going to lunch with you wearing your logo jacket. Picture them on the golf course playing the back nine with you. See them accompanying you on your next fishing trip. Visualizing success in this way is particularly useful when talking to prospects. As you develop these pictures in your mind, you subconsciously work harder to realize your goals.

WAY 19

Heroic Tales

Everyone loves stories of heroes. Heroic stories about how you and your crew have gone above and beyond the call of duty in serving your customers can be awesome sales tools to help convince prospects to become your customers. Collect and practice telling your own hero stories, because they carry more weight than all the advertising and promotion you can buy.

ACTION ITEM

Don't overlook the power of heroic stories that can work to your benefit. They should be happening in your company, so be sure to look for them and use them!

When Marie arrived to pick up a moving trailer, she was shocked to learn that the shop that was supposed to hitch the trailer to her SUV was closing for the day. Marie had rushed there after work and thought the shop would be open for another hour. But there had been a mistake in the shop's posted hours. The owner and one worker were still on hand when she pleaded her case, telling them that she was supposed to drive her son (and all his stuff) to college the next morning. Without the trailer, she could not move all the furniture and personal items he needed for the coming year. The business owner told Marie to pull her SUV in, and he and his associate stayed and got the trailer wired and ready to go. He apologized for the misunderstanding over the hours and helped Marie resolve her dilemma.

The business owner liked to tell Marie's story to his other customers, both because it made his business look good and because it reminded his staff that heroic deeds can and should be done every day. When the owner isn't around, this story encourages his employees to perform their own heroics to save and serve customers. This story will pay off for the owner for years to come!

Do You See What I See?

As Yogi says: "You can see a lot when you look." It's time to stop and look around your company to see how you're doing. Ray Kroc and Walt Disney both believed that no facility, building, vehicle, or object in their companies should ever appear to need cleaning, fixing, or painting. They believed that, if you address these needs routinely, your customers will always see a bright and shiny company that's up-to-speed.

ACTION ITEM

Make it a habit to take a walk around your company every thirty days and look at it through the eyes of your customers.

When Sparkle Pools decided to do an extreme makeover, the owner found the consultant he had hired sitting on a stump across the street from his business. When he went over to inquire what he was doing, the consultant said he was looking at the company as customers see it when they drive in. The exterior of the building needed a coat of paint and one of their signs had faded to the point that it was hardly legible. The perimeter of the building was choked with weeds, and the parking lot needed a fresh seal-coating. Overall, the property had been allowed to deteriorate and needed to be cleaned, swept, scrubbed, and painted. Think about the message that something like a badly painted wall or a handrailing that wobbles sends to your prospects and customers.

TAKEAWAY

Adopt the philosophy of Ray Kroc and Walt Disney and never let your customers see your business when it needs to be cleaned, painted, scrubbed, or fixed. Remember the power of first impressions!

WAY 21

Zero Defections

The best new customers are the ones you already have. While some customer attrition is inevitable, because businesses move away, sell out, go bankrupt, or confront other situations that you can't control, you should never accept the loss of a customer. Accept what you can't change, but never accept losses that are within your control. Your goal should be to have zero customer defections.

ACTION ITEM

Be a private investigator and learn from your lost custom-ers. Don't just accept the loss! Work like crazy to get them back. Remember, you once had a relationship with them, so go back and review what was successful in the past.

George, a seasoned and highly successful national sales man-ager, claims much of his track record is due to his hating to lose. He swears never to lose customers he values and wants to keep. When that rare event does happen, George launches his Operation Rescue and makes an all-out effort to regain their business. George believes that, to regain lost customers, he's got to become a private investigator to learn why they left him in the first place. That information yields valuable lessons that help him improve all his customer relationships, even if he ultimately loses the customer from whom he learned the lesson.

TAKEAWAY

Accepting customer attrition without trying to stem the tide can start a downward spiral. Learn to fight back, and renew those relationships!

Don't Turn Off Your Prospects

One thing we have learned in our research is that prospects and customers hate to see changing faces. They develop friendships and relationships and get to know people on whom they can depend. Personnel turn-over, or "churn," is very demoralizing for them. Prospects and customers accept the fact that people get moved, promoted, or transferred, but they hate to hear that they quit or were fired.

ACTION ITEM

Before dismissing an employee, ask yourself what impact it's likely to have on your customers. Consider transferring that person to another location and then, when the time is right, showing them the door. That way, your customers can accept the fact that they moved on normally.

Like it or not, you're really in the people business. You just happen to offer the products and services that you do. If you can organize, inspire, and energize a group of effective employees, the world is your oyster. It is your guaranteed key to success, regardless of the products and services you offer.

WAY 23

Pushy Prospectors

No one likes to be pushed. People love someone who will help them buy, but they really dislike someone who pushes them to buy, which they equate with pressure. One high-impact sales training seminar started by having attendees place a hand up against the hand of the attendee sitting next to them. Then the instructor gave the command to push. What happened when attendees pushed against the hand of the person sitting next to them? Their opponents pushed back!

ACTION ITEM

Become a super-sleuth. Ask, ask, and ask again, and you will find the hot buttons that trigger a customer's buying cycle.

One prospector completely changed the way he approached getting new customers when he saw this quote: "The secret is to get other people to do what you want done, because they want to do it." Start today with the mentality of finding a need and filling it, finding a problem and solving it, or finding an opportunity and taking advantage of it. This will help both you and your customers go from good to great! Without being pushy.

> **TAKEAWAY**
>
> *Always remember that people hate it when*
> *someone tries to sell them something,*
> *but love it when you help them buy.*

WAY 24

Don't Let the Fish Flop Away

Nothing is worse than finally catching a fish, getting it up on the bank, and then watching it slide back down into the water. When prospects finally request something from you like a sales catalog or a price quote, put them on your stringer before they can get back in the water. Don't waste time—time in which buyer's remorse can set in, or prospects can change their minds, or a competitor can beat you to the punch. You need to move quickly when a customer says "yes."

ACTION ITEM

Make certain that, when potential customers say "yes," you put them at the top of your list and service them until you get the sale. Focus your attention on these prospects until you make the deal.

When a salesman finally got a prospect to request information on a large wall cabinet full of electrical terminals, he was excited. He promised the prospect that he would be back the next week with product information, pricing, and availability. When he walked in the following week, he nearly had a heart attack. There sat a big display of electrical terminals the prospect had purchased from another sales rep who beat him to the punch. But he learned an important lesson. When customers say "yes," put them on the stringer and seal the deal. You have to move fast.

TAKEAWAY

When opportunity knocks, some people complain about the noise, while others spring into action. Which kind of person are you?

Your Way or My Way

At one time, K-Mart was the dominant retailer in America. Before they lost their way (and ended up bankrupt and were purchased at a bargain-basement price by Sears), they had surpassed Target, JC Penney, and many other retailers in market share. What was their secret for bringing in new customers? They built a system that was customer friendly.

ACTION ITEM

Think about how you can adapt to serve your customers, not how you can force customers to adopt your system.

Herb Wardlow was the architect who, for more than ten years, guided K-Mart as its president. He claims his secret for getting new business was incredibly simple: "Find out what your customers want and give it to them . . . and then some." Build a system to accommodate your customers' wants and needs, and then do the many extra little things that will get even more customers to come to you. If you do things their way, you are guaranteed to have delighted customers.

WAY 26

Help, Don't Sell

Think about the telemarketers who've called you, particularly during the evening. What did you do? Engage them in conversation or hang up? Most people hate telemarketers because of the intrusion factor. Selling has a bad image, so you have to learn to be a helper, not a seller. When you find out what customers' problems are and solve them, they will see you as someone who is truly committed to helping them, rather than someone who is desperate to make a sale.

ACTION ITEM

Make a card that says: "Help Before You Sell." Post it prominently around your office or desk as a reminder.

To say that purchasing agents are frustrated would be the understatement of a lifetime. Everyone who comes through their doors has one thing in mind—to get their business. If you want to be different, find out what their problems are. Find out what frustrates them. Find out what their competitors are not doing. Be seen as a helper, not a seller, and provide solutions. You'll be amazed at all your new business!

TAKEAWAY

---

*"Help" comes before "sell" in the dictionary—
and it should in what you do as well!*

WAY 27

The Power of Compliments

When was the last time someone gave you a sincere and meaningful compliment—something you knew was from the heart and that made you glow inside? If you're like most people, the answer is probably something like: "The last compliment? What year is this?" Have you ever met someone who complained about getting too many compliments or about being fussed over too much?

ACTION ITEM

Write down ten customer names, then write down one thing you could do to compliment each one. Put a smiley-face everywhere you look as a reminder that giving compliments makes people glow inside.

It was hard for people to figure out why they liked playing golf with Harry. He was an average golfer, but was it something he did that drew people to him and made them want to golf with him? Finally, one of his colleagues figured it out. When you hit a good golf shot, Harry complimented you: "Boy, you're really going to like that shot. What a great shot." When you sliced one, took a Mulligan, or heard the ball plop into the water, he supported you: "You know what? That's what I seem to do all the time." He had a way of minimizing your mistakes and maximizing your successes. In a world that is waiting to criticize, a compliment has incredible power. Find ways to give your prospects one compliment every time you talk with them.

TAKEAWAY

Beware when giving compliments to make sure they are sincere. People instantly know the difference between saccharine and sugar.

Become a "Yes" Person

Customers are in a hurry. Have you ever noticed how the post office capitalizes on that? For an additional charge, they will speed things up. If you want to send a large envelope in three to five days, you'll probably spend about fifty cents. If you need it there in two days, it can go Priority Mail and cost you around four dollars. If you just can't wait, they'll send it overnight for about fifteen dollars. What's the difference? The sense of urgency.

Can you do the same thing? Do you have opportunities to get your customers' work done faster for a small additional charge? Can you stop your normal processes and do it on a special-needs basis? More and more businesses are earning and justifying a priority charge for extra service. For example, your dry cleaner, printer, delivery service, tailoring shop, and caterer may all have two price schedules—one for regular service and one for express service.

ACTION ITEM

Identify where you can take advantage of offering something better, quicker, and faster for an additional charge. One manager has a sign in his office that says: "Good, fast, and cheap. Pick any two."

One Memphis electric-motor manufacturer solved an urgency problem that was constantly interrupting his production line by adding a same-day charge of 25 percent. He quickly found that customers didn't mind paying the additional charge if they really needed their items quickly, but they dropped their demands if it wasn't really necessary. His competitors refused to offer that kind of service. By developing two service schedules, he soon resolved his production-line problem. In addition, it earned him a lot of new customers who not only come to him for their emergency work, but who now come to him for their regular needs as well.

TAKEAWAY

Customers want options—even at a slightly higher cost. They will probably welcome the opportunity to get the service and delivery they really want.

WAY 29

Sell Your People First

It is amazing the risks many business owners and managers are willing to take by hiring people, giving them little or no orientation or training, and then simply throwing them out on the job. If your people aren't sold on you, your company, and your products or services, how are they going to convince your prospects? Training your people must be your first priority if you truly want to convince prospects to come aboard.

ACTION ITEM

Make it a rule that every new person joining your organization must be oriented to the values and beliefs of your company. Make yourself a checklist of the things they need to know and believe before you let them interact with prospects or customers. Create a training session that teaches them your philosophies and traditions.

Chicago-based Quill Corporation has a rule that new employees can't touch a telephone until they have been through several phases of training. They learn about the history of the company, about its culture, rules, and policies, and about its procedures and traditions. They must be able to demonstrate that they are convinced Quill is a great operation before they ever go near a phone. The management is adamant that they will not let employees talk to prospects or customers until they know about and believe in the company.

WAY 30

Fix the Problem

If you've ever called on a potential customer and unknowingly walked into a hornet's nest, you know how critical it can be to defuse difficult situations. A small dose of training can cure a large case of unhappiness. It can also help you avoid an argument that you will rarely, if ever, win.

ACTION ITEM

Learn how to defuse angry customers. The key phrase is: "What can we do to fix the problem?" Remember, if your customers are not satisfied with the solution, you could easily lose them. It's not an issue of pride, so be sure to keep your ego out of your responses.

Fortunately, when Brian got blindsided by an angry engineer, he knew how to handle the situation. After he assessed the problem that had upset the engineer, he asked an important question: "What can we do to fix this problem and make you happy?" By avoiding a confrontation with the customer that would lead to both parties becoming defensive, he was able to get to the root of the problem and resolve it, turning an unhappy complainer into a happy customer.

TAKEAWAY

You may win an argument, but you could lose the customer. Do you want to be right, or have the business?

WAY 31

People Are Funny

In the early days of television, Art Linkletter hosted a hit show called *People Are Funny*. Prospective customers are also funny— as well as prejudiced, predictable, and picky—especially when it comes to the appearance of the people with whom they do business. Your appearance can turn them on, turn them off, or even permanently shut down your chances.

ACTION ITEM

Learn how your customers want you to look and dress. Develop a standard that fits with their vision and remain consistent.

Before you grow a beard, get a tattoo, or let your hair grow out, take inventory of how your prospects may feel about and react to your appearance. Why start campaigning for new business by turning your prospects off before you even get a chance to establish a relationship with them? Is this a blinding flash of the obvious to you? Never underestimate the power of appearance. Do your research, and conform to the expectations of your customers.

TAKEAWAY

People want to do business with people who are like them. They avoid doing business with people who are not!

Inspire New Hires

When being offered a job, every applicant wants to know about salary. Good employers understand that, in addition to answering that question, it is inspiring to brief new hires about when they can expect future pay reviews. For example, new delivery drivers may be told they will have a pay review in ninety days, and again at six months.

ACTION ITEM

Make certain you set specific pay-review intervals for your sales force so they know what to expect. Accelerate the raise scale for your most successful employees.

When Chris hired new staff to help him win new customers, he knew that their attitude, work ethic, and dependability were important to his organization. When Judy got off to a running start, and Chris got outstanding feedback about her work, he used a powerful strategy to inspire her and ensure that she would stay with him. At thirty days, Chris called her to say that all her coworkers were bragging about her performance. Then he reinforced the key behaviors he needed from her. "Judy, you have exceeded our expectations for a new person on the team. Therefore, I am going to exceed your expectations by giving you your pay raise today instead of in ninety days. We will review your pay again in six months." Chris understood that, while praise is nice, it doesn't buy groceries! Do you think Judy will do back flips for Chris in the future? You can be sure of it.

WAY 33

Respect Their Time

We live in an age where people feel incredible pressure to get things done immediately, both in their businesses and in their personal lives. We are all trying to accomplish more in less time, and feeling pressured to cram forty-eight hours' worth of activity into a twenty-four-hour day. You can send a huge message to prospects by consistently showing them that you and your company have a sense of urgency about meeting their needs, and that your organization will hustle to serve them.

ACTION ITEM

Identify the key areas in your company where a sense of urgency is important, and show it to your prospects and customers every day.

While standing in line at the local post office, one patron commented to another: "I'm always amazed that they only have two lines open when they have so many customers, and both of the clerks on the counter seem to be in slow motion. Their demeanor, their body language, and the excessive time they're taking with customer conversations tells me that they really don't care." While I'm sure that the post office has some very competent and capable employees who understand their customers' needs, they've generally been labeled as having poor customer service because, all too often, that's what they provide. Don't allow your company to be like the post office. Develop a sense of urgency that reflects your customers' needs.

TAKEAWAY

Your prospects are watching you, and nothing is more powerful than proving you have a sense of urgency about serving them.

Target Your
Prospects' Interests

The old saying "different strokes for different folks" is certainly true of your prospects. They all will have their individual interests, hobbies, or passions. Your goal is to learn what those are—fishing, hunting, golf, collecting antiques, woodworking, restoring a house, or building vintage cars. The secret is to know what interests your prospects, so you can become interested in the same things. When you know what flips a prospect's switch, you can look for interesting things you can pass along on that subject.

ACTION ITEM

Keep an inventory of what interests your customers and look for those things every day. It can be anything—from an article in the newspaper to a special television show, from a brochure on a new product to an advertisement about a new service.

When one salesperson learned that her customer had just gotten a new puppy, she zoomed right in on that subject. She stopped by a local pet store and found a free quarterly newspaper chock-full of ideas, stories, ads, and articles on the training, nutrition, and care of puppies. She wrote a quick note to her prospect and sent the materials along in the mail. On the next call to that customer, they had something to talk about. The customer was so impressed that the salesperson had taken that kind of interest in him that he soon became one of her most loyal customers.

TAKEAWAY

Prospects are flattered when you recognize and share in their interests, hobbies, or passions. Capitalize on your common ground and use it to build a personal relationship.

WAY 35

All Buyers Are Liars

A group of prospects meeting with a sales representative at a Colorado steakhouse were all complaining that their steaks were overcooked. When the waiter came and asked whether everything was okay, all the people who had just been complaining said: "Sure, everything's fine." As the waiter walked away, one said: "I wouldn't come back to this place again if you paid me." How many times have you lied to a waiter or waitress and told them everything was okay when, in fact, the service or meal wasn't good? Remember that customers have two kinds of objections—the ones they tell you about and their real objections.

ACTION ITEM

Remember these questions: What can we do to earn your business? and What can we do to get your business back? When you put prospects in a position of helping rather than whining and complaining, they will be more likely tell you the truth instead of putting you off.

Ben was a loyal buyer from a warehouse distributor. One day, something went wrong and he stopped doing business with them. He went from being a customer back to being a prospect. When a new sales rep was assigned to call on Ben, he knew that getting the truth about what had happened could be difficult. When he sat across from Ben in the office, he asked one simple question: "What will it take to win back your business?" He put Ben in a situation where he could be positive and actually share what the distributor needed to do to get back in his good graces. Instead of allowing Ben to criticize his company, the sales rep allowed him to help find a solution.

WAY 36

Brag, Brag, and Brag Some More

Will Rogers said: "Get someone else to blow your horn, and the sound will carry twice as far." If you have associates with whom you work who are exceptional at their jobs, it can be a tremendous asset when you're trying to convince customers to join you. From a newspaper ad that features their picture and a story about them, to your personal tribute and stories when you're making sales calls, there are many ways to highlight quality people to help you get new customers. It's a powerful tool.

Identify your top people and the three qualities that make them outstanding so you can tell their stories in print, in marketing, and in person.

Jack wasn't just a good machinist who built high-performance engines; he was a great machinist! Many people labeled him a quality fanatic who was obsessed with the shop's reputation. His own reputation was awesome, and the amount of work in his shop showed it. Think about how you can turn an associate's stellar reputation into a sales tool. Think about how you can make the Jack in your organization bigger than life. People want to be around successful people, and you can take advantage of the great reputations in your organization.

TAKEAWAY

Sometimes a person's reputation is as valuable as the person. Find out who the stars are in your company and make sure to highlight their talents and skills.

Pay Attention to Individual Needs

Customers are people, too! If you pay attention to their needs in addition to offering your products and services, you can benefit a great deal. Like it or not, your business is probably not that much different from your competitors', and you need to recognize that. By making a concerted effort to address your prospects' individual needs, you motivate them to find you in the crowd. Capitalize on the features that make you different.

ACTION ITEM

Teach everyone your plan to meet your customers' emotional needs by promoting this easy formula: EN1 = Emotional Needs First.

The owner of a beauty salon was failing in his attempt to build his customer base. He had many competitors in the area, and the simple fact was that they offered many of the same services. He began to identify the individual needs of his customers with a program to get each person comfortably settled. He made sure customers knew what the salon's schedule was going to be and who was going to work with them. Then he offered a choice of beverages and snacks. At the end of each visit, he gave customers a small gift to take home, and he always made sure to tell them how important they were and remind them to come back again.

WAY 38

My Name's Not Bud

How serious are you about attracting new customers and cultivating long-term relationships with repeat buyers? If that's your intention, beware of the tragic blunder many companies have made in trying to win my business. I've been called Bud, chief, sweetie, honey, honey-pie, lover, and everything except my actual name. While this may seem trivial to many, psychologists say that a person's name is, to each of us, the sweetest sound. Start by making sure that your associates have your customers' names available so they can use them to help build relationships. Getting and using customer names is a very simple tactic that your competition may overlook.

ACTION ITEM

Get your associates into the habit of using proper names instead of nicknames. Getting and using people's names is a good habit. First, we make our habits, then our habits make us.

Membership retailer Sam's Club ran a campaign about using customer names. On the back of every cash register, the company posted the word C-H-A-N-T—a reminder to all employees that Customers Have A Name, Too. In fact, they instituted a rewards program to remind employees of the importance of identifying people by their names. Do you think you can get better at doing that, Bud?

> **TAKEAWAY**
>
> *In survey after survey, customers complain about being treated like a number, so make sure that your company doesn't do that.*

Beware of Agitators

There are a lot of great, friendly, and fun people to do business with in America. But for some reason, there also seems to be a small group that delights in agitating, debating, and instigating trouble at every step. It seems as if their goal in life is to push your buttons, belittle your company, find fault with your products and services, and tell you that your competitors are better than you are. The secret is not to let these people get to you. After all, if you don't want them to get your goat, don't let them know where it's tied.

ACTION ITEM

Find a book about dealing with difficult people. Read it, and teach the techniques to your staff.

The best time to deal with agitators is before you encounter them. Start by making a decision that you are not going to react instinctively. Instead, decide how to prepare and respond to these doom-and-gloom people. Learn to harmonize with their objections and tell them that you can understand their feelings. If they know how to push your buttons, they'll just continue to do it. If they don't know what sends you into orbit, they'll just give up and stop agitating you—and pick on someone else.

*Don't let the critical few destroy your
attitude about dealing with the majority,
of whom many are a pleasure to serve.*

WAY 40

Label What
Differentiates You

We live in a world where every business yells and screams: "We are different. We are better. Choose us." In reality, it's usually nothing more than old wine in new bottles. You need to commit to being truly different with a program that prospects can see. Then label what you do. The label is a daily reminder that sends a message to prospects, customers, and employees alike. Marketing professionals call it a "value statement." You may recognize it as a tag line.

ACTION ITEM

Define your value statement so that your employees can internalize what you want them to know. Label as many things as you can with it—letterhead, pens, posters. This can serve as a daily reminder to capitalize on what makes you unique!

A company called Image One wanted to define their uniqueness, so they came up with a rather clever tag line: "The Image One Way, The Only Way." This helps their prospects and customers identify their values and ideals. The company then educated its staff about its new tag line and made sure that everyone understood the philosophy it entailed.

> **TAKEAWAY**
>
> *You have to name it to claim it, so decide what makes you unique and slap a label on it. A copyright can help, too!*

WAY 41

Do Something Different

Prospects just love to be wined, dined, and solicited by potential suppliers, because it means they have been accepted and are valued. Acceptance is one of the key motivating factors in life, but in many areas of customer service, it's no longer enough. You have to do something different, bold, and creative to show your customers that they are valued and accepted. Find something unique, fun, and/or mysterious to convince your prospects to become your customers.

ACTION ITEM

Put your creativity to work on developing fun, interesting, and unique ideas to involve your prospects and customers. Organize a team to help come up with some good ideas for special events.

Vicky was an award-winning sales manager who invited her top ten prospects to a unique customer presentation. They each received a series of three mailings inviting them to join her on the dock at a local reservoir to take a leisurely tour on her boat. Hors d'oeuvres, drinks, and a bit of fun were built into the event. The creative mailings went on to explain that ties would be cut off at the neck and anyone not wearing shorts might be thrown into the water. At the appointed hour, Vicky was amazed that all ten prospects arrived at the dock and climbed onto her boat to spend the afternoon schmoozing and learning about her products. Within weeks, all but two became customers.

WAY 42

Be Creative

Your competition can be very predictable. They will probably do what they've always done. Very few people are really creative enough to break through the clutter and get a prospect's attention at little or no cost. Remember that nobody notices normal, so sometimes you have to break the rules to get through to prospects and build relationships with them.

ACTION ITEM

Get your team together and brainstorm some things you can do to break through. Consider leveraging holidays and special events. Be creative and reach out to prospects. Don't just wait for them to come to you.

If you run a small to mid-sized business and can have face-to-face contact with your customers, try this great idea for reaching out to your prospect list. On a hot afternoon, load up a cooler full of Popsicles, ice cream bars, or cold lemonade and go customer to customer serving everybody a nice cool treat. I doubt anyone has done it for them in the past, and it's unlikely anyone other than you will do it again in the future. It's a great opportunity to hand people something free and refreshing to remind them that you truly want their business.

TAKEAWAY

Most people are looking for something different. They don't know what they want, but they'll know it when they see it. Make sure they see you!

WAY 43

Go in Naked

We've repeatedly pointed out that making cold calls and developing new customers is not for the faint of heart. Cold-calling requires a tough hide, a strong spirit, and a persistence very few people have. That's why the failure rate in selling is so incredibly high. One of the key strategies for achieving success is not to look like a salesperson out to shove merchandise down a prospect's throat.

ACTION ITEM

Learn to go in naked and to ask questions. That's the only way you're going to learn the needs, problems, and opportunities of your prospects. This will allow you to go back later and make that presentation with your two briefcases full of sales information.

Sandy was an attractive, enthusiastic, and sincere sales rep when she hit the road for the very first week. On Friday, she reported back to her sales manager that her sales productivity that week had been zero. He was baffled why she had had no success, because even a dog with an order form tied around his tail can occasionally get somebody to take it off and fill it in. By making sales calls with her the next week, he identified her problem. She went into unknown prospects armed with two briefcases full of literature that screamed: "Here comes a salesperson! Here comes a salesperson!" Prospects ducked and avoided her like rabbits getting out of the way of a shotgun. She had to learn to go in naked on those early calls and learn about her prospects long before she ever tried to sell them anything.

WAY 44

Believe It or Not

Believe it or not, prospects and customers will stretch the truth, especially when they tell you their side of an incident, mistake, or problem they had while trying to do business with you. Before you go on a rampage, accusing your staff of stupidity or mismanagement in handling the customer, be sure to get their side of the story first.

ACTION ITEM

Think like a judge and give everyone a chance to be heard before arriving at a decision. Often you will find that the customer is wrong.

When Harry went to the warehouse looking for Debbie, who had filled an order incorrectly for a customer that morning, he was smoking mad. They had tried and tried to get this customer's business for a long time and now, just when they had closed the deal, Debbie screwed it all up.

But Harry listened to Debbie's side of the story before he went ballistic. Not only did she believe she had filled the customer's order just as he had wanted it, she still had his notes to back her up. Sure enough, Debbie was right, and the customer was trying to save his ego by blaming her. Harry learned to get all sides of the story before making a judgment. He complimented Debbie and told the office to close the prospect's line of credit. He didn't want a new customer who had already proven he would lie to cover himself. That day, Debbie grew a foot taller because of her boss' trust in her!

TAKEAWAY

When your employees are right, stand by them, even if it upsets a prospect or customer. Your associates will respect you for it. After all, right is right!

Try Something Different

Email is a great communication tool if you can get your prospects to respond to you. Getting them to answer your emails, however, may take creativity and humor. People often don't respond because they are busy, on work overload, or simply don't know what to say to you. Try something different to catch their attention and get them to email you back. Humor can be a good way to prompt a response.

ACTION ITEM

Get creative and use humor when emailing some of your more reluctant prospects. But make certain you target only prospects who will respond favorably to your humor.

One sales rep experimented with different kinds of emails for prospects who failed to respond to him. He settled on something like this:

Dear Mr. Jones,

I've stopped by several times to see you and tried to get you on the phone to share an exciting proposal. Since I've not heard from you, I thought maybe one of the following things had happened:

1. You've been dragged into the outback by wild dingoes and are being held hostage.

2. You won the lottery and now have millions and millions, and you no longer need to talk to me.

3. Wild women have discovered you are single, and you had to go into hiding to escape the mobs that are after your body.

If you get a chance, or you come back from one of these three situations, please email me back. Let's plan to get together to share how we can help you make some extra money.

Thanks!

TAKEAWAY

If you do what everybody else does, you'll get the same results everybody else gets—which are generally pitiful. Try something different.

Customize, Customize, Customize

In a restaurant survey, 74 percent of respondents said the number one thing they liked to have when eating out is a salad bar. Why? Because they can make their salads their own way. They can have a little of this, a lot of that, and some of the other. They can make their salads exactly as they like them, with just the right mix of ingredients, dressing, and croutons for them. In today's world, people want a product that is truly customized—one that is as individual as their personal tastes.

ACTION ITEM

Think about how you can customize your products and services to fit your prospects' needs. People don't want one size fits all.

When Sue confronted her boss as a new employee, she asked him: "Do you know what's standard around here?" When her boss said "no," she answered: "Nothing. Every customer wants something different. They want it their way." Her boss looked at her and said: "You're right. Why don't we do it that way?" Think about the first thing clothing stores do when you buy a nice suit—they tailor it to fit you. They shorten the sleeves, move the buttons, take a little out of the coat, and hem the pants or skirt. Suddenly, you've got the product you want, detailed just the way you like.

WAY 47

Little Things with Big Payoffs

Potential customers often comment on little things—little things that can result in huge payoffs if you listen, change, and react to their feedback. Listening, and demonstrating that those changes are important, sends a huge message about how much you care.

ACTION ITEM

Make it a rule that everyone within your organization or company write down any feedback that could be considered important by management.

A local library had just completed a multimillion-dollar renovation and addition. It was beautiful and well done, right down to the button that automatically opened the door for people with special needs. However, as a gentleman in a wheelchair approached the door, it became obvious that the doorway was too narrow for his power wheelchair, which barely slipped through. They needed to put an automatic opener on the second half of the door so that both parts opened to accommodate visitors in wheelchairs.

The gentleman made his way to the desk to explain the problem to the librarian, but she had all the empathy and sympathy of a drill sergeant. Her body language, her facial expression, and her reaction to his comments sent the message that she could not have cared less. Do you care about the little things that bring big results from your potential customers? Listening to them and making even minor changes and adjustments can send an important message about your willingness to accommodate their needs.

Showing empathy and sympathy is the best way to convince customers that you are serious about meeting their needs.

Be Different

Joel Weldon has famously said: "Figure out what everybody else is doing, and don't do it." To be recognized in the clutter of today's market, you've got to figure out a better way, a different way, and a more affordable way to keep telling your story. One of the ways to do that is to look at the changes going on in the marketplace.

ACTION ITEM

Study your competition and the marketplace, then devise new and innovative approaches that your competitors are not using. Try going back to snail mail to be different.

With the popularity of the Internet and email, there have been some dramatic changes in the ways people communicate. Some of the things left behind that can pay off for you are your fax machine, letters, postcards, and the good old telephone. Those things get attention today precisely because people have almost stopped using them. Consider how you can update the fax, the postcard, the letter, and especially the phone call to keep in touch with prospects and customers. This can be a different and better way to break through the clutter. The opportunities are everywhere.

TAKEAWAY

*If you always do what you've always done,
you'll always get what you've always gotten.
You have to make changes to win customers.*

WAY 49

Do What Others Don't

While some messages are ideal for email or fax, there are some things that should never be sent that way. It's all too easy to cop out on sending a proper thank you note, invitation, or confidential message. By simply sending an email, you also send the message that it's not important enough or confidential enough for you to use a more traditional means of communicating.

ACTION ITEM

Make sure you have the materials on hand—cards, stamps, addresses—to communicate in more traditional ways. This makes it easy to do something that others don't. You've got to systemize these types of mailings, or they won't get done.

In most areas of the country, there are stores that feature paper goods and discount greeting cards. In fact, some of them are so affordable it is almost ridiculous. So stock up on thank-you cards, invitations, birthday cards, and note cards with no message inside. Get in the habit of recognizing people, inviting them to special events, thanking them for what they do, and celebrating things like birthdays or anniversaries. By using traditional mailing methods, you'll be different, because most people these days simply send emails. Prospects will recognize your extra effort and reward you for it. Remember, you're building relationships. You should do personal things for people with whom you have a relationship!

> **TAKEAWAY**
>
> *Get in the habit of using traditional means to communicate that other people have abandoned, and you will stand out in the crowd.*

Learn from Chameleons

We want to do business with people who are most like us. This is where your appearance and behaviors can work for you—or against you. Learn from the chameleon, who can change its appearance to match the color underneath or behind it. It can go from green to black to blue to suit its surroundings. How can you change to be more like your customers?

ACTION ITEM

Study your customers, and then become a chameleon. What do your customers wear for a casual lunch as opposed to a formal dinner? What do they wear for presentations or meetings or celebrations?

Nido is a highly successful banker, entrepreneur, and professional speaker. His closet features outfits for every occasion, from meeting with a CEO to blending in with a group of technical people. You can bet he will look most like them. How does Nido do it? He studies what other people do. What do they wear? What shoes do they wear? He may even call ahead and talk to a client to get some feedback on appropriate apparel.

There's nothing funnier than to see someone show up in a suit and tie when everyone else is in blue jeans, or to see someone show up in blue jeans when everyone else is in a suit and tie. Learn from Nido, and work to look like your customers so they will want to do business with you.

WAY 51

Beware of First Appearances

We all know that you never get a second chance to make a first impression. But there's another part to that rule: You never get a second chance to judge people if you judge them wrongly in the first place. If you judge your customers' ability to buy, or their willingness to become long-term customers, based on their appearance or their body language, it's easy to make a huge mistake. You can't tell what's on the inside by what's on the outside, and you can't tell people's net worth, their ability to spend money, or their ability to borrow money based on their appearance. The best practice is to assume that everyone may be a prospect who can buy, and then sort them out as you ask questions and get to know each one.

Learn not to make snap judgments based on appearance. Ask some key questions to qualify prospects rather than just depending on how they look.

The owner of a small high-performance auto shop had been having a tough day when a young customer came in and began to ask prices and availability on a page-long list of high-cost items. Somehow the owner managed to keep a smile on his face as he quoted price after price. However, inside he was telling himself: "This is a waste of time. This guy could never afford to buy this stuff." After pricing many thousands of dollars worth of merchandise, the young man looked at the shop owner and said: "Okay, I'll take it." To which the owner responded: "You'll take what?" The customer replied: "Everything you just quoted." With that, he pulled out a roll of $100 bills to pay for the items. The owner learned a great lesson that day. Never judge a person by what's on the outside, and never assume prospects can't or won't buy based on their appearance.

TAKEAWAY

There's no way of knowing for sure whether the person with whom you're talking is a pauper or a millionaire. The best practice is to let them qualify themselves rather than run the risk of judging them incorrectly.

Be a Super-Sleuth

You can never know too much about a prospect to whom you'd like to sell. The more you learn, the more likely you are to win over that potential account. There is no excuse for being uninformed in today's information-rich society, where you have resources like your local library and the Internet.

ACTION ITEM

Think of yourself as a detective building a case. You must convince prospects to become customers, so be sure to do your research first!

When a consultant was invited to meet with Flagstar Bank to consider doing promotional work for them, he downloaded every page from the company's web site and learned everything he could—from its mission statement to its philosophy of customer service, from its growth plans to its financial performance in recent years. When he walked in to meet with Flagstar management, he was armed and ready to discuss where they'd been and where they were going.

WAY 53

Inspired Employees = Dedicated Customers

I encourage you to buy a copy of my book, *No Nonsense: Inspire Your Staff*. Not because we want to make a sale, but because it will help you to grow a group of excited people who are ready, willing, and able to make your company a success. Can you think of anything more important? The real secret to inspiring people is to get them involved and give them a reputation to live up to. Show them that you have high expectations of them, and then watch them follow through and prove you right.

ACTION ITEM

Analyze each of your people and decide what unique gifts they have and what things they do well.

Jerry, the owner of a mid-sized company, hired a comptroller named Mae. He soon began calling her his human computer. She was indeed a genius at organizing and running his office, and he enjoyed working with her so much that he bragged about her to everyone who would listen. Frequently, Jerry gave tours of his business to prospective customers, and he always made a point to take them to Mae's office and introduce her. She became a partner in helping grow the business and took great pride in her work. Give your people a great reputation to live up to, and then get out of their way and let them do it. It's a successful formula that will not fail you.

> **TAKEAWAY**
>
> *People become what they see themselves to be. When you lift them up and put them on a pedestal, they will perform to that level.*

The C-Y-A Factor

More than one sales rep knows the agony of defeat. And sometimes defeat comes from failing to get permission before taking an action, which can result in anything from a small dose of criticism to a big dose of being fired. Adopt this simple rule: When in doubt, check it out. Get permission before you proceed on anything that may backfire on you later!

ACTION ITEM

Make it a rule that, if your gut reaction gives you any concern, you will make time to check things out. You may even want a customer to initial or sign off on what you're about to do so you can C-Y-A (Cover Your . . .).

An advertising agency once placed an ad for Wal-Mart on the West Coast without running it by Wal-Mart management first. It was far outside the style of what Wal-Mart typically did, and customers and prospects alike were insulted. Ultimately, the agency was fired and lost a very lucrative account. If they had gotten the ad cleared with Wal-Mart management, even on a local level, they probably would still have the account. Unfortunately, they're now out doing a great deal of prospecting for new customers. But they've learned an important lesson—always check with the appropriate authorities before making any big decisions.

WAY 55

The Best Prospect Ever

Prospecting for new customers can be hard work. It can be expensive, and it can eat up your time like a hungry goat in your front yard. The best prospect has always been—still is, and always will be—the one who contacts you. When potential customers contact you, you start with people who know they have a need or want, who are ready to buy, and who are giving you a vote of confidence by reaching out to you first.

ACTION ITEM

Do anything you can—as long as it's legal and ethical—to get prospects to call you. Call, poke, push, pull, incentivize, motivate, stimulate, remind, inspire. Whatever it takes.

Renee, a response-and-marketing consultant from Florida, believes that there are three important prospecting principles to remember at all costs:

1. Your success will be determined by the quality and quantity of your prospect list.
2. Your prospects must hear from you a minimum of every thirty days to maintain top-of-mind awareness.
3. Getting prospects to call you means making them multiple offers.

TAKEAWAY

When customers call you, they see themselves as welcome guests. When you attempt to sell them, they see you as a necessary pest.

Stick Like Velcro

We all have common desires, such as being wanted, needed, and accepted. When you make emotional connections with your prospects and get to know them as people, you go a long way toward establishing rapport with them. It is easy to forget that prospects have lives beyond the office. If you can make an emotional connection with them, stick to them like Velcro and never lose it!

ACTION ITEM

Write yourself a note to remind you and your employees that people buy from people, then learn to "inner-view" your prospects so you can get to know what's inside them.

When Steve attended a family reunion, he was amazed at how quickly the years seemed to disappear as he talked with his long-lost relatives. That was because their common interests about the family made it easy to pick up where they had left off years before. Your prospects are ready, willing, and waiting to establish a relationship with you if you take the time to "inner-view" them. That means getting to know where they were born, where they went to school, their hobbies, their families, their pets, and their greatest accomplishments. Learn to establish at least one topic with each prospect that you can continue as a dialog each time you connect. Find common ground, and they will become not only your customers but also your friends.

WAY 57

Whatever It Takes

Good prospectors maximize their time and multiply their efforts by using affordable resources to call on their customers. Develop a philosophy of using W-I-T (Whatever It Takes) to gain and retain prospects and customers. You can have a huge impact on your success if you keep top-of-mind awareness with your prospects, especially those on your Top 10 list. So do whatever it takes to maximize your prospecting efforts and win new customers.

ACTION ITEM

Go to your local post office and get a stack of priority envelopes, mailers, boxes, and labels. You can access postage costs on the Internet, so you can handle everything from your office. Then routinely communicate with your prospects using whatever it takes.

One easy way you can reach out to customers is through your friendly mailman. Think about how you can use Priority Mail, which is affordable, available, and cost-effective, to send special messages to your prospects. Priority Mail gets attention; it says that what's inside the package is very important. Prospects pay attention to it because it is different from the pile of regular mail, which is probably just bills and advertisements. If you send them a Priority Mail package once in a while, they'll be impressed, and they will know you are serious about wanting their business. It's a great investment, because it works.

> **TAKEAWAY**
>
> *You can multiply your impact on prospects by using Priority Mail and the thousands of hardworking postal carriers across the country.*

Love Those Journals

If you are like most people trying to gain new customers, it is likely you serve a wide range of businesses and occupations. For example, your prospective customers may include butchers, bakers, candlestick makers, and many others. One of the best ways to learn more about your prospects' interests is from their trade and professional journals. Every industry and every trade has specialty magazines and journals that contain a treasury of tips, tricks, trends, and other information you need to know to be able to talk to your prospective customers.

ACTION ITEM

Visit the kinds of businesses you want to learn more about. Most of them get some kind of trade journal and will be glad to share their reply cards.

When new employees come to work for Rodney, the very first thing he does is to give them the reply cards out of the various trade journals associated with his business and have them subscribe. Most trade journals are absolutely free and are supported by industry advertising. He encourages his employees to make time each month to go through them and keep up with developments in the various industries. His office currently gets about a dozen different trade journals, and they are all well used. Nothing flatters prospective customers more than knowing that you have taken the time to learn more about what they do, what their interests are, and what challenges they face.

WAY 59

Do You Qualify?

One hard-and-fast rule in sports, and in competing for customers, is that you can never win if you're always playing defense. Consider turning the selling process on its head and approaching customers to see if they qualify to do business with you. By screening customers to see if they qualify, you can activate one of the great motivational principles and build an eager desire within your prospective customer base.

ACTION ITEM

Make your customers want your services. To make this principle work, you've got to be able to stack up the benefits of what you're offering.

One financial planner has developed a track record for helping his clients earn a great return on their money. The number of referrals sent to him is something most salespeople can only fantasize about. He's in the enviable position of being able to tell prospects that his services are not for everyone, and that they need to meet to see if they are a good fit. He actually interviews prospects to see if he will allow them to come aboard as customers. By the time the interview is over, most prospects are begging him to take on their investments. Can you turn the selling process on its head and qualify your customers?

TAKEAWAY

The more exclusive an item is, the more people want it. Make your prospects want to be your customers, and develop an exclusive client list.

Before You Open Up

If your business attracts customers at specific opening times, like my favorite coffee shop that opens at 6:00 a.m., nothing sends a stronger negative message than walking in the door and watching employees scramble to get their act together. If the coffee's not made, there's no money in the register, and several employees are late, that's a poor way to start the day.

ACTION ITEM

Make it a point to be open and ready when you are supposed to be. That's just meeting customers' expectations. Then go on to delight them with your products and services.

Consider investing in having one or more employees come in early to get everything ready so that, when you open the door, you're ready to serve customers. Customers should be able to depend on you to serve their needs and offer them the products they want, all with delightful customer service. It's the professional way to run a business, and the small investment in additional payroll will definitely pay off.

Being prepared gives your staff the confidence to smile at customers. It also lets customers know that you're prepared and ready to serve or help them.

WAY 61

Tell and Sell

I'm a confessed nut about prospecting at little or no cost. One important strategy is to have your name and contact information on everything you print, sell, make, take, or give away—anything that could possibly direct a prospect back to you. The best strategy is to have your website visible on everything from pens and notepads, to calendars and tape measures. If you leave these items with prospects, either purposely or accidentally, they will eventually notice your contact information and either call you or check you out online.

ACTION ITEM

Teach your staff that nothing is to leave your business without having your contact information on it—web site, email address, or phone number. Just make certain prospects have a way to reach you!

One prospect couldn't remember our name and phone number and had unfortunately lost our business card. Luckily, he found a pen that I had left there several years ago that had our web site on it. He was able to visit us online and reach us through our contact information. Since then, he has become a huge customer and is likely to spend many dollars in the future. We would never have gotten this account had we not taken the step of being visible and giving people a way to contact us. You have to remember to tell and sell to meet prospects and make customers.

> **TAKEAWAY**
>
> *A funny thing happens when you don't promote yourself. Nothing!*

Keep Your Links Current

One great and easily affordable way to reach prospects is through email. Not only is this a convenient way for customers to reach you, but it can also give you the opportunity to respond in a well-thought-out manner. Email can happen on your own terms and your own schedule, without forcing you to be quick on your feet. You can take the time to gather price quotes, efficiency statistics, or other data that might come in handy when speaking with a prospect. But you can't do any of this if your email addresses and web links aren't current. There's nothing more frustrating than clicking on a link and going nowhere.

ACTION ITEM

Keep your email contact information current. When you discontinue an email address, consider keeping it up and checking it daily. Provide a link to your current address until you are absolutely confident that no one will attempt to contact you through the old address. You can also retain the domain name and have the ISP redirect email to your new web site or email address.

Unfortunately, more than 20 percent of all the contact links on the Internet are broken, so when you click on the link, it either doesn't connect or gets bounced back. Some businesses confuse, and inadvertently sabotage, their prospects by making it hard for them to make contact because they frequently change their email addresses. When you drop established email addresses, you close the door on prospects, which could make you lose the sale of the century! Don't let this happen to you.

TAKEAWAY

Out of sight means out of mind. Make sure that prospects can find you whenever they need to.

Leave a Trail

You've heard the old adage about leaving a trail of bread crumbs to lead you back home. That's what you should be trying to do with prospects. Leave a trail that reminds them of your company and that you want their business. This can be anything with your name and logo on it, from pens to baseball caps, from memo pads to golf balls. The long-term goal is to give reminders and create an outpost in your prospects' minds. If you leave bread crumbs for them, they will eventually find their way back to you.

ACTION ITEM

Find a source for logo and identity items. Buy up a variety of items and get them out on the highways and byways where your prospects operate.

A busy association executive had met with a prospective insurance provider numerous times. He failed to notice that each time this agent called on him, he left a small gift. One day, he looked at the top of his desk and discovered that he had a memo holder, a leather address book, a large desktop calendar, a pen holder, pens, rulers, and more—all with the insurance company's name, logo, and phone number on them. When his current insurance program hit a speed bump and he had to find another vendor, it was easy to decide whom to call. Their name and phone number were everywhere. Not a bad investment for some logo identity items that were left behind.

TAKEAWAY

In today's over-communicated world, where it is nearly impossible to get your advertising message out to customers, this concept is a winner that you can implement with little or no hassle.

Learn from the FBI

The Federal Bureau of Investigation is known coast to coast for their 10-Most-Wanted List. Each week, they review and update the list, removing people who have been captured and adding people who warrant it. You can use the same idea to focus your time, energy, and resources on your best prospects by having your own 10-Most-Wanted list

---

ACTION ITEM

Make a Top 10 list and develop the weekly discipline to update it. Be sure to make assignments so that your staff knows who is responsible for each prospect on the list.

Terry, a very effective sales manager, believed that, if his salespeople tried to sell to just any old prospect, they would probably do a poor job and not sell anything. He learned that he had to get them focused on their best sales opportunities. Each Monday morning, he required his associates to complete a new Top 10 list for action that week. He also required them to write beside each item the action or activities they were going to take that week to turn that prospect into a customer. By having them focused, and having a copy of their Top 10 action plans, he kept them on target to go after their best prospects.

WAY 65

Keep Top-of-Mind Awareness

What do other people think of you? At age twenty, you worry about what everybody's thinking about you. At age forty, you don't care what people are thinking about you. And when you get to age sixty, you find out they weren't thinking about you in the first place. The goal with all your prospects is to keep T-O-M-A (Top-of-Mind Awareness).

ACTION ITEM

Take every opportunity to maintain T-O-M-A (Top-of-Mind Awareness) with your customers and prospects. Try something at least once a month. And don't forget them while you are on vacation.

A sign in a store said: "We wouldn't worry about what people think of us if we realized how seldom they do." Keeping top-of-mind awareness is an awesome task, but it can be accomplished. For example, on your next vacation, take along a set of labels or the addresses of your best prospects. While you're sun bathing on the beach or sitting beside the pool, send them some I-wish-you-were-here postcards. Every tourist area has them. They are affordable, and they're a fun way to communicate and keep T-O-M-A with your prospects.

WAY 66

The Proof of the Pudding

The proof of the pudding is not in the tasting but in whether people return for a second helping. You can get anyone to try a bite of your favorite recipe, but if they don't care for it, getting them to take that second bite is going to be tough. The same is true with prospecting for customers. Getting new customers is simply a function of your willingness to spend on promotion and advertising, and to do cost-cutting and giveaways to bring them in the door. If you do all that, you can get the new customers. The question, however, is whether you can get them back again.

ACTION ITEM

Develop a system to track repeat business and customer longevity. This will help you identify why customers leave and why they come back.

While visiting a new church in our area, I was interested to notice that, although this beautiful facility had been there for many years, there weren't enough parishioners at the Sunday morning service to fill more than a few pews. Something was wrong. At the end of the service, the pastor asked us to sign a visitor logbook. The book was filled with pages showing that visitors had signed in, gone out the door, and never come back. The problem with this church was not that they weren't getting prospects; it was that they weren't converting them to customers. Keep your focus, not just on the first sale, but on the second and all future sales. If you don't get repeat business, you're never going to be successful as a prospector, because repeat business is the proof of the pudding.

WAY 67

What about Tomorrow?

The best way to ensure that customers will return to your company in the future is to make sure that your associates understand the importance of delightful customer service, because it's the only way to guarantee that customers will return.

ACTION ITEM

Get your group to brainstorm what it will take to get customers back for the next sale. Reinforce the idea that the next sale is just as important as the current one, and they will be sure to treat each customer with respect.

The owner of a quick-lube/oil-change center found a masterful way to convince his employees of the importance of customer service. He had them ask themselves one simple question when serving customers: "Is what I'm doing today going to bring this customer back tomorrow?" They had the sale for today. The issue was to get customers to come back in the future. This savvy business owner realized that fixing cars was only part of their job.

TAKEAWAY

Always remember that, when you fix a problem,
you have to be sure to fix the customer.

WAY 68

Your Elevator Speech

There's an old saying that you never get a second chance to make a good first impression. When someone asks who you are and what you do, how do you respond? You need to have an elevator speech that, in sixty seconds or less, tells people who you are, what you sell or what you serve, and why they should do business with you. You may only get one chance to make that good first impression.

ACTION ITEM

Script your elevator speech, and make sure everybody in your company can recite it word for word so they're all on the same page.

A business owner was interested in changing local zoning laws. He met a member of his local legislature as they got on the elevator to go up to the conference room. The legislator pushed the button for the twelfth floor and, when the door closed, turned around and said: "What do you want from me and what can you do for me? Tell me in sixty seconds or less." Amazingly, this business owner was prepared. He had a well-defined answer and, by the time the elevator stopped on the twelfth floor, the legislator was ready to help him, and also to get the benefit of having him as a supporter in his upcoming reelection campaign. Can you tell people in sixty seconds or less why they should buy from you?

> **TAKEAWAY**
>
> *When someone tries to slam the door, don't put your foot in it. Stick your head in so you can keep talking.*

Point Out the Problem

If you've watched television infomercials, then you know how problems can be exaggerated and made bigger than they really are. In fact, most infomercials are for products that solve problems that most people don't even recognize!

ACTION ITEM

Define the problem, then work to find ways to make the problem common knowledge. Once your prospects know that a problem exists, they will be eager for your solutions.

Have you ever heard of halitosis? Although the condition of bad breath has been around for ages, the word to describe it was not well known until the early part of the 20th century. The term "halitosis" was made popular by the salesman who invented mouthwash. He found a problem, advertised and exaggerated it, then sold the solution and made himself a fortune. When you find a problem, be sure to point it out to your prospects. Your solution will be a breath of fresh air!

Go After Lost Customers

Sometimes the best customers to get are the ones that got away—the ones who defected and went to the competition. They just may have found that they aren't as happy as they thought they'd be. Your continued efforts to win them back could result in regaining a good customer, perhaps an even better customer than you had before. Lost customers often are simply waiting for you to invite them back.

ACTION ITEM

Keep a lost-customer list and keep track of your efforts to win them back.

The owner of a dental laboratory lost a big customer who represented more than 40 percent of his regular business. Although he tried to reach out, the customer failed to return his phone calls. After much debate, he decided to try something a little different. He bought a sympathy card and wrote a personal note to the customer. He explained that he wasn't sure what had happened or why he was unhappy, but said it was a shame that they weren't doing business together anymore, because he believed they were good for each other. He offered his sympathy that the company would have to do business somewhere else. He sent the card and soon got a return phone call. The customer wanted to sit down and talk, and soon returned as a loyal client. Don't give up on lost customers.

TAKEAWAY

You know what a lost customer can be and how your relationship can improve if you make the effort.

WAY 71

Free Still Works

Of all the powerful words you can use in selling your marketing message, the word "free" is still at the top of the list. In fact, one marketing magazine noted in a article that free food and drink still brings out more people than a great guest speaker or a high-impact seminar topic. We all love to get something for nothing.

ACTION ITEM

Give prospects a free meal. Always inspect the place where you plan to take them in advance and arrange for a quiet corner or a table where you won't be interrupted. It's worth the planning.

If you have potential high-value customers that you've not been able to win over, consider offering them a free gourmet meal. Include these key things in your invitation to help them accept:

1. Make sure they understand that they are under no obligation to join you.
2. Assure them that they will be your guests and that you are going to pay.
3. Promise there will be no high pressure sales pitch while dining. Making them feel safe will encourage them to say "yes."

WAY 72

Out of Sight, Out of Mind

If it often feels to you as if we spend our lives standing in line, you're right! Of the average seventy-eight-year life span, it is estimated that up to five years are spent waiting to be waited on. No one likes to wait in line when it's not necessary, and no one likes to see employees in your place of business doing things that aren't related to direct customer service. Although sometimes these other tasks are necessary, try to get that work done out of sight of your customers. The people standing in line won't become upset if they see every associate working busily to serve their needs.

ACTION ITEM

Teach everyone to stay out of view when they are not directly serving customers. Perhaps more important, empower them to decide that customers are more important than what they are doing, and get them to help out with customer service. Customers just don't understand why they cannot be waited on.

The fast-food industry has gotten a black eye in recent years and their customer service rating has slipped in each annual survey, because customers often see twenty people working behind the counter—cooking, scrubbing, or cleaning—and only one person waiting on them. If you have situations where people need to work on things other than serving customers, get them out of sight so they'll be out of mind.

> **TAKEAWAY**
>
> *Customers don't want to be served very soon; they want to be served now. The business that eliminates waiting in line will be the one that wins the new customers.*

Email—Friend or Foe?

Electronic mail has become the most prominent method of communication in our modern society. Even the post office is feeling the effect of email. The volume of letters has dropped significantly, although the population and the number of businesses continue to increase. Email can be a great tool for prospecting, or it can be your worst enemy.

ACTION ITEM

Collect every email address of every prospect, and create an email series so powerful that your customers will look forward to it every week or month.

One corporate executive claims that she gets over 200 emails a day, and it is about all she can do to keep up with them. What's even worse is that she estimates 70 to 80 percent of them are unnecessary. That means that you have to be careful about using email. Here are three simple rules:

1. Make sure the subject line of each message is personal for the person to whom it's going. Many emails are simply deleted without being opened because they scream SPAM.

2. Never send broadcast emails without getting the permission of the people you put on your list.

3. When you've got something of benefit to the recipient, don't be afraid to send it by email, but make your message short and sweet.

TAKEAWAY

When used correctly, email can be your greatest prospecting tool. Used without caution, it can become your worst nightmare.

WAY 74

Keep the Lights On

It's unlikely that your business can justify offering 24/7 customer service, and it's possible that your customers don't even need or want that level of help. But today, there are simple and affordable ways to show your customers they aren't stuck when your door is closed and the lights are out.

ACTION ITEM

Offer a variety of options—from your web site to your telephone to your emergency services—to let your customers know that, when the lights are out, you are still ready to help them. Find out what your competitors are doing in your industry, and then do more than they are. Adopt and adapt their ideas and strategies to your needs.

Arriving at a major chain drugstore, one customer was exasperated to find it closed. Then, on the door, she noticed a sign directing her to the nearest twenty-four-hour pharmacy. She was thrilled. What can you do during nonbusiness hours to help your customers? Hire an emergency phone-answering service? Establish a cell phone number or beeper to call in an emergency? Set up a 24/7 help line to answer their questions and hold them off until you open? And what can you do when the phone rings after hours? Rather than let customers just hear it ring, how about an answering machine that tells them when you can serve them?

TAKEAWAY

We are no longer an 8-to-5, Monday-to-Friday society. People have diverse schedules, and they often look for services when many traditional businesses have turned out the lights and gone home. Those who can accommodate them will win and retain their business.

One Magic Word

When you deal with customers, the magic word is "happy." It's virtually certain that you are eventually going to encounter a prospect or a new customer who is unhappy with you, your products, your services, or your company. Knowing how to deal with emotional issues can turn upset customers into loyal buyers and be the pivotal point of either losing their business or winning their hearts. Find out what will make your customers happy and give it to them whenever you can.

ACTION ITEM

Always use the word "happy" when dealing with prospects and customers. It is a critical concept that is understood by most people around the world, regardless of the language in which it's spoken.

When a telephone service manager encountered a customer who was upset, he listened attentively and then asked the magic question: "What can I do to make you happy?" The customer first said that he believed he deserved a $400 credit against his bill for the time his phone service was down. The manager quickly agreed and said: "Will that make you happy?" The fellow then said that he wanted to get some service people out to his home to have his phones fixed by four o'clock. The manager said: "My very best people are already en route. Will you be happy if your phones are up and running by 4:00 PM?" The customer said he wanted one more thing, an apology. With that, the telephone executive apologized for the errors they had made in serving him. He knew that the secret formula for dealing with upset people is to ask the question: "What will make you happy?" Then, whenever possible, settle the dispute on their terms.

TAKEAWAY

Negotiate happiness on your customers' terms and, when you agree to what they want, they will feel empowered.

WAY 76

Quality Speaks Volumes

For a number of years, a woman in a television commercial for Hanes underwear used the slogan: "It doesn't say Hanes until I say it says Hanes." The ad was a huge success in selling their undergarments. For many years, quality control in America deteriorated so drastically that overseas competitors stole a large portion of our market share. Today, however, we're back and doing better than ever. But the painful lessons we learned about building a reputation for quality products and services has been expensive.

ACTION ITEM

Make a decision today that you're going to drive your company toward superior quality. Then communicate that goal to customers and prospects. Quality is the cumulative effect of many choices.

The late W. Edwards Deming was respected worldwide as a proponent of quality. He said that quality didn't really cost anything, but was in fact a profit center. Quality products result in fewer rejects, less maintenance, less down-time, extended performance, more enjoyment of use, and an increase in customer loyalty.

TAKEAWAY

There will always be a top-end buyer who's willing to pay a premium price for quality products and services.

Keep Up with Technology

We live in an ever-changing world. By the time you buy a new computer or a piece of equipment, it's already out of date because there's a better one coming down the assembly line. The challenge is to keep up with the latest in technology and equipment to maintain your position in the marketplace. The secret is to budget a fixed amount that will allow you to keep up and remain a state-of-the-art operation. Staying on the cutting edge will give you an advantage when turning prospects into customers!

ACTION ITEM

Set up a review process for evaluating your technology against current standards. And don't forget to budget for upgrades! Technology = productivity = competitiveness = great prospecting.

A printing shop in Las Vegas has a policy of investigating any and every piece of new equipment that comes on the market. If they have a printing press that is only a year old and a new and better one is offered by the manufacturer, they investigate it to see if it's truly a better product. If it is, they immediately sell the one they have and buy the one that offers them the latest and greatest in features and benefits. Because they have the best in equipment and people, they also attract the best customers. Most of their printing is for Fortune 500 companies' annual reports and for the Las Vegas gambling casinos who want nothing but the best.

TAKEAWAY

The world is moving on whether you do or not. The secret is to keep up with the latest technology to best serve your customers.

WAY 78

Is Your Image Working for You?

Look around your company today—the buildings, the vehicles, your offices, your signage, and your trucks on the road. What kind of message are you sending to your prospects? How would you rate yourself as you appear today? Sad and definitely needing improvement? Average or typical when compared to your competition? Or would you rate yourself as outstanding? It's important to take the time to analyze what your image is to determine whether it's working for or against your long-term goals.

ACTION ITEM

Take inventory of your company's image and set a goal that you will no longer accept average. While being average may not work against you, being above average or outstanding will definitely work for you. You want to stand out in the crowd like a rose among thorns.

Mike's Car Wash is a highly successful regional group of carwash facilities. The appearance of their facilities is not typical or average, but it is definitely working for them. It begins with their huge colorful signage, their manicured lawns, their beautiful flowers, and their spotlessly clean and meticulously well-kept facilities. When you swing your car around to start through the conveyor belt, it is given an extra treatment on the front and rear to steam-clean bugs and tar away. You are even greeted by two smiling employees in nothing less than shirt and tie. Can this really be a car wash?

> **TAKEAWAY**
>
> *Make sure your image is working for you; if it isn't, it's working against you. Why start the day by swimming against the current?*

Don't Take Anything for Granted

One huge problem in getting new customers is falling into the trap of complacency. If you go in unprepared, and the competition follows you with a great dog-and-pony show, guess who gets the sale? You will be left asking what went wrong, and the competition will walk away with the customer.

ACTION ITEM

Ask yourself, am I too complacent? What do I really need to do to sell this prospect?

A Las Vegas sales rep had an opportunity to make a presentation to a large organization. Because the prospects knew him and he knew them, he debated what kind of sales presentation to make. Finally, he called one of his mentors who sat on that organization's board and asked what kind of approach he recommended. The wise man said: "If you had never met this group, what kind of presentation would you make?" The sales rep responded that he would have a full-blown PowerPoint presentation, a custom book with all the details, and a room set up to sell the project. That is exactly what he did, and he had a very successful meeting. Always prepare as if you have never met your customers or prospects, even if you've done business with them before, and you'll be successful every time.

WAY 80

Beware of Prescriptions without Diagnoses

Imagine seeing a new doctor who, without saying a word, begins to write out a new prescription for you. No medical history. No vital signs. No context. Would you pay for that visit or take that medication? It's very doubtful that you would feel comfortable doing so. Getting a prescription without a diagnosis is called malpractice!

When a plumbing wholesaler was desperately looking for ways to increase sales and get new customers, he asked his will-call sales staff for suggestions. They said the customer-service area needed to be spruced up. They needed a new counter, better uniforms, improved signage, and a nice place for customers to come in and pick up their orders. The owner did exactly what his people recommended, but sales didn't go up at all. Why? Because it wasn't important to the customers!

So the wholesaler personally went out and made calls on his plumbing contractors and asked them what was critically important to them. They explained that having the right pieces in stock was what they valued most. If just one gooseneck for a sink installation is missing, a plumber is shut down and can't finish the job. Filling the order was what they valued most. The wholesaler decided to guarantee every contractor that each order would be filled 100 percent within twenty-four hours. The program was a huge success, and his sales volume skyrocketed. Why? Because he prescribed what his customers needed.

Make It Easy to Buy

In recent years, Americans have started paying more bills with credit and debit cards than they do with cash or checks. It's a turning point that signals to businesses everywhere that they should be flexible with their accepted methods of payment.

ACTION ITEM

Take inventory of how customers want to pay you. If you don't have the credit cards or check guarantee service they need, get them today! This will make it easy for customers to do business with you.

There's a sign in a Las Vegas casino that says: "How would you like to pay? We accept gold dust, gold bars, Mastercard, Visa, American Express, Carte Blanche, Discover, and Diner's. We will take a company check, a personal check, or your traveler's check. . . . Heck, we even take bad checks. And of course, we will take cash." Everybody has a good laugh when they see that sign, but they remember one thing. This casino makes it easy to do business.

How are you making it easy to conduct transactions, request service, or order inventory? Will you accept gold dust and gold bars? Do you take all major credit cards? If you make it easy for customers to buy from you, you'll convert prospects into customers faster than ever before.

WAY 82

Make Them Feel Safe

Dr. Carla Morgan has pointed out that virtually all potential customers you approach have been lied to, taken advantage of, and probably cheated at some point in their lives. They have probably heard lots of promises that never came true. By addressing their need for safety and security, you increase the probability of winning them over. Making customers feel safe and secure when doing business with you is an important strategy in prospecting.

ACTION ITEM

Get others to help you analyze where potential customers may feel risk, pressure, or obligation, and design a prospecting program that will overcome their objections.

In convincing one of his most skeptical prospects, one sales rep found that the word "no" had a big payoff. As he communicated his desire to do business with prospects, he assured them again and again that there would be no risk because of his absolute, positive guarantee. There would be no selling, because all he wanted to do was point out how he could help. There would be no obligation, because they would have the right to say "no" with no hard feelings, no further pressure on his end, and no embarrassment. He never put prospects in a situation that would be awkward for them. And it worked, because he converted that skeptical prospect. Make your customers feel safe. Take away the risk, manage their fears, and watch what happens.

> **TAKEAWAY**
>
> *Like it or not, fear is always a factor. Making people feel safe and secure is a very basic principle for getting new customers.*

Loose Lips Sink Prospects

During World War II, the phrase "loose lips sink ships" was used in propaganda posters to remind the American people not to divulge secrets. The same holds true in dealing with potential customers who are willing to share their confidences with you. Just make a promise to yourself that, when prospects and customers share confidences, you will not divulge that information to anyone.

ACTION ITEM

Remember the rule that the only way two people can keep a secret is if one of them is dead—don't ever share confidences.

When Bob called one of his key suppliers to discuss several internal problems he had, he opened the conversation by asking that it remain confidential. Then he revealed that he had been having some theft problems inside his business. Together, he and his supplier were able to formulate a plan to help Bob deal with the theft. More important, they cemented a relationship based on trust, which is the ultimate compliment anyone can give you. The supplier assured Bob that no one would be told about what was going on. He gave his word on that. Could a prospect or customer trust you in that same situation?

Build Trust

Trust is the most essential ingredient in all really great relationships, both personal and professional. Unfortunately, trust must be earned over time by consistent performance. It's very rare that customers will trust you on the first day and with their first transaction.

ACTION ITEM

Make a rule that a promise made is a promise kept. Remember that your word is your bond.

Retailing giant Sam Walton recognized the value of trust as he built the Wal-Mart empire. He said: "If I could stand trust at the register, I would be home free. The reality is you must earn a customer's trust one customer, one transaction, and one day at a time." One thing you can do to gain more trust is to keep your promises and follow through, and then point it out to your prospects or customers. For example: "Bill, I told you I would have these for you today, and here they are." Or: "Mary, I promised I would call you back on Wednesday, and today is Wednesday." When you do the right thing, make an issue of it and wave your flag in the air. It helps you accelerate the process of building trust.

TAKEAWAY

Trust is more fragile than an egg, and you need to protect it every day, with every sale, and with every prospect or customer.

WAY 85

Falling Out of the Dumb Tree

Do you believe you can build a successful long-term business that will attract new customers by lying, cheating, or deceiving customers? Do you believe your customers fell out of the dumb tree and hit every limb on the way down? That seems to be the way many businesses approach their customers, but they don't last long. Customers are not as dumb as many businesspeople think they are. Abraham Lincoln once said:"You can fool all of the people some of the time, and some of the people all of the time, but you cannot fool all of the people all of the time."

ACTION ITEM

Always tell the truth, the whole truth, and nothing but the truth. Build your reputation on that.

A business owner was finally able to buy a really high-quality copier. He was excited about the many things it would do because he had a variety of needs in his office. One of the staff's first projects was to create postcards for a mailing they hoped to get out that day. As they fed the postcard stock into the machine, it jammed and refused to print or copy anything. It was exasperating! When the copier service person arrived and they explained the problem, he looked at them and said: "Our salesperson told you that? He told you this machine would run postcard stock? Sorry, but it won't!" How long do you think that salesman will succeed when he tells falsehoods?

WAY 86

Consider Name-Dropping

We see everyone from sports greats to rock stars, from movie idols to political celebrities attempting to sell us all sorts of items and ideas. There is real power in celebrities or sports stars trying to convince us that a specific product or service is good for us. When Oprah features a book on her TV show, it is guaranteed to sell a quarter of a million copies almost immediately, simply because she has so much credibility with the book-purchasing public. Never overlook the power of influence in your attempts to win customers.

ACTION ITEM

Ask yourself who on your customer roster could help you influence others to come aboard. Then ask for their help in developing testimonials.

If you ask, many of your existing customers will give you testimonials about how your products or services have helped them. They may even allow you to use their photographs along with their quotes. Think about how you can use testimonials, name-dropping, or perhaps a list of your existing customers to influence others to join you. But proceed with caution, and remember: When in doubt, check it out. Be sure to get your customers' permission before using their photographs, names, or testimonials.

TAKEAWAY

If you're not convinced of the power of other people's influence, ask yourself why a book on Oprah's list sells millions of copies just because it has her stamp of approval.

Freebies Are Hard
to Turn Down

Getting something for free is hard to resist. Regardless of your prospects' loyalty to your competitors or their reluctance to consider you and your advantages, freebies can often break through. Think about what you can do to get their patronage with offers that are almost unbelievable.

ACTION ITEM

Think of free or inexpensive things you can do that are within your budget. Get your team together and come up with some creative ideas.

When a Phoenix manufacturer wanted to entice a number of prospects from around the country, he planned a very special open-house weekend at his facility, including a celebration, golf, and other fun times.

Each prospect was sent a package containing an engraved invitation, a personal letter from the CEO, an agenda that oozed with excitement, and a certificate good for two coach round-trip air tickets to Phoenix. Everything was paid for by the host. It was a huge success, and almost all the prospects flew to Phoenix. In time, many of these prospects were converted into loyal customers. There's something about show-and-tell and bricks-and-mortar that pays off, but the freebie was the real catalyst that made it work.

> **TAKEAWAY**
>
> *The word "free" will always be the #1 motivator of people, both personally and professionally.*

WAY 88

Advertise Creatively

If you do any radio or television advertising, then you know it's incredibly expensive, generally ineffective, and often a poor use of your promotional money. But it doesn't have to be that way. You can break through the clutter, get people's attention, and build name recognition by doing something a little different. We call it problem-solving with a dose of humor. People love to be entertained, and they love to see a problem followed by a solution. When you tickle their funny bones, they will remember you.

ACTION ITEM

Any time you're creating ads, whether for print or broadcast media, try to use this formula: Problem + Solution + Humor = Impact.

One of the best examples of the problem, solution, and humor formula is an ad by the Hertz car-rental company. A gentleman walks up to a shabby car-rental establishment and explains he'd like to rent a Bronco. The shady employee behind the counter quickly fills out the paper and takes his money. Then the camera switches to this poor guy on top of a horse bucking, kicking, and giving him a hard time. Unfortunately, he's been duped. Then the camera switches to Hertz and shows how they go above and beyond to deliver a real Bronco (manufactured by Ford) and provide customer service like no one else.

TAKEAWAY

If your advertising is just like everyone else's, you'll probably get about the same results everyone else does. Break through the clutter with a healthy dose of creativity and humor.

Claim Those Free Dollars

Promotion is more important than ever these days, and most manufacturers and distributors have funds available to help you go after the prospects you so desperately need, using a technique called "co-op promotions." Some pay up to 90 percent of the actual cost! And you aren't limited to using only radio, TV, or print ads. Creativity can get that same chunk of cash transferred to your account to do things like mailings, trade shows, customer luncheons, golf outings, a fishing contest, or a weekend escape. Be creative and go out and claim these free funds.

ACTION ITEM

Catalog every major brand and customer you deal with and aggressively go after any "co-op" funds that may be available. Make yourself a sign that says: "Claim It or Lose It." Because, if you don't get those funds, someone else will!

Harry was an aggressive retailer who loved to promote his business and go after prospects, especially with other people's money. He kept a log of every supplier and pushed every manufacturer about what spiffs, co-ops, and promotion money they had available. He just asked and asked and asked again. He was relentless. He befriended many of the sales reps who called on him and learned if they had discretionary dollars. By being friendly and asking often, he got the promotional money to go out and get new customers.

> **TAKEAWAY**
>
> *Remember, if you don't ask, you'll never get!*

One Magic Question

Everyone who wants more customers longs for a magic formula to bring in more business. Be sure to ask customers the magic question that is virtually guaranteed to bring you more business: "If I can find a way to provide the products and services you need, will you consider buying from me?"

ACTION ITEM

Write out this 1-2-3 formula, and pay attention to the answers. Use this magic formula when prospecting for customers.

Dan, a lifetime prospector who successfully sold everything from oil filters to investments in oil wells, pioneered a three-step process that worked like magic to turn prospects into new customers.

1. Find out much as you can about your prospect on a personal level to connect and build rapport.
2. Probe and dig to unearth what your prospect needs.
3. Ask the magic question: "If I can find a way to provide the products and services you need, will you consider buying from me?"

This formula helped Dan sell millions of dollars of products and services in a variety of businesses and industries.

TAKEAWAY

Many seasoned and successful salespeople claim you need to ask your way to success.

Always Deal
with a M-A-N

We've all had times when we thought that we had a prospect ready to become a first-time customer, only to be blown away by the disastrous words "We can't afford it," or "I have to get permission to buy it," or "Sorry, but we don't really need it." To avoid these deadly sales-killers, you have to make sure that you're always dealing with a M-A-N—someone with the Means, the Authority, and the Need to buy.

ACTION ITEM

Make sure in advance that your prospect has the means (the money or the credit), the authority (the right to sign a purchasing agreement), and the need (a use for your product or services) to become your customer.

Mary Anne had called on a manufacturing company's purchasing agent several times and had established a good rapport. She was confident that, by sticking with it, she would get their business for the industrial tools, cutting drill bits, and hand tools that they needed. Only after several months did the buyer finally explain that his wife was also a representative of an industrial tool company, and he just couldn't buy from anyone else.

Mary Anne had been going down a dead-end path because she was not dealing with a M-A-N. She had not qualified the prospect to make sure that he had the means, the authority, and the need to buy.

TAKEAWAY

Don't try to sell clothes to nudists, meat to vegetarians, bibles to atheists, or guns to peace activists. This will just waste your time with unqualified prospects.

WAY 92

Yes, No, and Maybe

Nothing contributes more to the demise of salespeople and prospectors than the word "maybe." Everyone understands "yes, it's time to go." Everyone understands "no, it's time to quit." But the worst situation is when prospects string you along with the word "maybe." It's somewhat like when the fish keep nibbling all day long, but you don't catch anything. At the end of the day, you have no fish, no bait, and no daylight left. You've spent your entire day waiting around for a "maybe" to become a "no," which is just a waste of your time. Learn that "maybe" is not an acceptable answer.

ACTION ITEM

Don't hang on too long, wasting your resources. Know when to quit fishing and find another lake.

Andy says he understands "yes" and "no," but "maybe" is the word he's had to learn to deal with most often. After a reasonable period of time, he will do virtually anything to get a customer to move in one direction or the other. He actually sees it as a benefit when customers say "no," because he can take them off of the "maybe" list and move on.

> **TAKEAWAY**
>
> *Customers will often string you along, and there is a huge benefit in getting them to say either "yes" or "no." Don't be afraid to take a knockout punch to find out whether it's worth investing your time and energy.*

Bigger Is Better

If you operate a small or mid-sized business, there are probably times when your prospects need to see you as a Goliath in a land full of Davids. Sometimes you need to use perception and illusion to appear bigger than you are. In many prospects' eyes, bigger is better.

ACTION ITEM

Find some creative ways to make your outfit look more like Goliath and less like David. But be careful—most illusions are uncovered at some point.

Jack operates half a dozen meticulously clean delivery and service trucks that feature eye-catching graphics. His graphic designer suggested a bite-size idea that has convinced prospects he must surely be operating a large fleet of vehicles. He began numbering his trucks with different numbers on the right and left sides, because no one ever sees both sides of a truck at the same time. For example, on the first truck, it says Unit 6 on the left side and Unit 8 on the right side. On the next truck, it says Unit 10 on the left and Unit 12 on the right. Then Units 14 and 16, 18 and 20, and 22 and 24. When you see his trucks coming or going, you are led to believe that he has the largest fleet in town, when in reality he operates only six vehicles. How can you use a similar subterfuge to look bigger to your prospects?

WAY 94

Networking

Networking can be one of the most powerful tools you have for opening dialog with potential customers. Have you ever tried reaching out to a prospect you know you can help with your goods or services and been stopped dead by gatekeepers? Maybe it's time to consider who you know. Try reaching out to someone who can help you break down the walls separating you from an important sale.

ACTION ITEM

Do your homework to find out who your colleagues, coworkers, friends, and family know. Almost everyone knows someone who may be a prospect.

Jack had tried several times to reach the president of a successful restaurant chain to talk about his unique flat-rate maintenance program for their commercial heating and air-conditioning systems. He could offer the company better service at a better price, but he couldn't get through.

One Sunday morning at church, Jack overheard another parishioner mention that he knew the president of the chain. He approached him and asked if he would introduce Jack and his company to the executive so he could tell him about their great service. The very next morning, Jack got a call from his friend telling him that the prospect was expecting a call, and would welcome setting up a meeting to discuss how Jack could help his company get better service at lower cost.

TAKEAWAY

Who do you know who could open a door for you?

One Size Never Fits All

One size will never fit all. You need to see all prospects as individuals who need a program custom tailored for their needs. Great prospectors don't have rigid policies and procedures. Instead, they empower their people by giving them flexible guidelines to follow.

ACTION ITEM

Tailor everything you do to individual buyers and you'll win a lot of customers. Do you have rigid guidelines, rules, or regulations that you can't adjust to fit your customer's needs? Remember that one size does not fit all.

The more Mary Anne called on Charlie, the more she realized he had the potential to be a high-volume customer. But so far, all she had been able to get was an occasional sale. Walking into his facility one day, Mary Anne noticed a piece of equipment that she had sold him several months before stuck under a workbench. When she inquired about it, Charlie explained that, while there was nothing wrong with the equipment, it simply didn't work for his application. She immediately went over, pulled it out from under the workbench and told him she was going to take it back and give him a credit. He quickly explained that she really didn't owe him a credit, because the sales period had run out. He admitted that he had bought it in error and not returned it early enough. Because Mary Anne's company offered her guidelines and not hard-and-fast rules, she knew it would be smart to take the item back and give Charlie a credit. That one gesture pushed him over the edge, and he immediately became one of her highest-volume buyers and a most loyal customer.

TAKEAWAY

So many people are afraid of being taken advantage of that they fail to realize that 98 percent of customers just want a fair deal and to be treated as individuals.

WAY 96

All's Fair in Love and War

Everyone has heard the old proverb: "All's fair in love and war." For this quick idea, we add a third term: "All's fair in love, war, and competition for customers." If you are going to compete in the marketplace, you must know what your competition is doing. There are three kinds of people who compete: the active, the reactive, and the inactive. Only the active will win the competitive wars in the days ahead.

ACTION ITEM

Be active! Ask all your friends, employees, sales reps, colleagues, and industry contacts to bring you materials and keep you up to date on what the competition is doing.

If you ask Dorothy what is going on with her competitors, not only can she tell you, she can show you. She has a file on each competitor, and she makes a daily effort to keep up with what they are doing. She has a network of informants who keep her advised and bring her catalogues, price sheets, promotional information, and the kinds of details she needs. There is no way you can have a good strategic program to get new customers unless you know what your competition is doing. If you are inactive or reactive, make a decision today to become active.

TAKEAWAY

Fairness is in the eye of the beholder. Do whatever it takes to learn what your competition is doing—as long as it's honest and morally right.

Do You Know What They Know?

In today's high-tech world, it is impossible to know what your prospects know without doing some research. There are some grave dangers in making assumptions. It's dangerous to get caught up in the jargon of your product or service and assume your customers know the language. But it's also dangerous to talk down to clients who have a great deal of industry knowledge. The best rule is to assume that you don't know, and then find out.

ACTION ITEM

Make a 3 x 5 card that simply says: "Speak Their Language!" Keep it visible around your work space as a constant reminder.

When a sales manager called a prospect, he began to explain his products and services by conveying the most rudimentary facts and figures. The problem was that the gentleman on the other end of the call was an engineering professor in the area of interest they were discussing. The more the sales manager talked on, the more upset the prospect became. Finally, he ended the call because he felt insulted. A safe question to ask is: "How familiar are you with this subject area or this product or service, and what would be helpful for you to know?" Let customers tell you what they want to know and then pick up the conversation from there.

> **TAKEAWAY**
> _____
>
> *You will rarely get in trouble when you let customers tell you what they need to know.*

WAY 98

What Gets Repeated

For this quick idea, we borrow a basic principle from personal-influence psychology, which was pioneered by the late M. R. Kopmeyer. Its key principle is: What gets rewarded gets repeated. Reinforce a positive action with a compliment, a comment, a note, a small gift, or anything that may stimulate someone to do it again. Build on the successes you have with prospects. As you reinforce the behavior you want, they will do it more often.

ACTION ITEM

Make yourself a poster or card to remind yourself: "What gets rewarded gets repeated." Build on positive behavior and, as much as possible, overlook the errors, sins, and omissions of your people. Then watch what happens.

Christy was a new executive assistant to a hospital administrator when he handed off a real mess. He asked her to take his pile of papers, notes, and scraps and turn it in to an executive report that he could turn in to the Board of Directors. She dug in and spent a tiresome day taking his jumbled mess and turning it into a professional report. When she left it on his desk, he came out bubbling with excitement about what she had accomplished. He told her that the next day he was buying her lunch. Christy learned that, when she does well, her boss acknowledges and rewards her, which makes her want to do even more. It's a win-win situation for both of them.

> **TAKEAWAY**
>
> *Catching people being good means overriding our natural instinct to criticize, condemn, and complain.*

Traditions Are Sacred

It is important in your prospecting efforts to communicate the traditions of your company that prospects will respect and admire. These traditions should be held sacred by you and your associates, because they embody the ideals and philosophies that your company holds. After all, everyone likes a touch of class. It can help build spirit and encourage prospects to see you and your company as having value and substance.

ACTION ITEM

Decide on a few things that are sacred to your company and protect them. Tell your prospects what these values mean to you and what they should mean to them.

On a fact-finding mission to South America, one CEO was overwhelmed by how much the local culture respected its temples, statues, and religious artifacts. The executive quickly found himself being very careful about where he stepped, what he touched, and how he handled himself. He had unconsciously adopted the culture's respectful attitudes, and found himself behaving similarly. Then he realized that he could apply this to his own business. When he went back to his office, he worked with his staff to create a set of traditions and values that his prospects, customers, and associates could see and appreciate.

WAY 100

The Puppy-Dog Lick

Many people have become dog owners as a direct result of the law of unintended consequences. At some point, they picked up a warm, cuddly puppy who gave them a big, loving lick across the face, and they were sold. Without ever intending to own a pet, they suddenly found themselves dog-owners. The puppy went home to become a part of the family.

When a suburban homeowner with several acres of beautiful woods went out to buy a chainsaw, he was really disappointed with what he found in most stores. The display saws looked cheap, were tied down, and did not appear capable of doing a tough job. Finally, he hit a home run when he stopped in a store that had a huge display of chainsaws and people who could explain about each and every one. But the puppy-dog lick came when the sales rep invited him to go out back with the chainsaw and try it out. After cutting several limbs from a tree trunk they used for testing, he was sold. They made a sale, and everyone else lost out on a prospect that day.

TAKEAWAY

All the advertising in the world can't compare to one good personal experience.

Don't Give Them a Reason

Have you ever met people who wouldn't change their minds or wouldn't change the subject? That is the exact principle one highly successful entrepreneur used in building a number of profitable businesses. His philosophy was: "Never give a customer a reason to go somewhere else."

ACTION ITEM

Become the competition. Never send your customers elsewhere for the things you should have.

It was just a few minutes after 6:00 a.m. as customers began to enter a local bakery and espresso bar. To their great dismay, they were greeted by an announcement that the coffee-and-bread store had run out of coffee. Customers either had to drink soda or water, or go somewhere else. So many of them went out the door and down the street to a nearby shop that had coffee. Unbelievably, there was a twenty-four-hour supermarket just a few blocks away where the store employees could have gotten a variety of coffees and met their customers' needs. They literally forced their regular customers to go elsewhere for that first cup of coffee. This is industrial-strength stupidity.

WAY 102

What Do You Sell?

When Jack Trout and Al Reis wrote the popular book *Positioning: The Battle for Your Mind*, they argued that your business name is crucial. It should be the shortest distance between you and your prospect's mind. Make sure your business name states clearly what you are selling.

ACTION ITEM

If you can't change your business name, consider working hard to define the tag line below it so that it tells what you do and why customers should come to you.

Review these actual business names, and try to identify what they sell:

Tuesday Morning

A. J.'s Close

21st Amendment

The Sugar Plum Tree

Bounce Back

Tulip Tree

Priscilla's

Mad Dog's Place

Amerispec

Juniper Services

If you hit on even one or two, it would be a miracle. Does your business name really tell who you are and what you do? If not, maybe it's time to change.

> **TAKEAWAY**
>
> *Put your ego aside and decide that the most important thing you have is the name of your business.*

Everything Matters

What's important to that new customer you've been trying to win over from your competitor? Everything! Getting new customers is about doing a few big things—and hundreds of small things—better than your competition. We call it managing your T-C-E, or Total Customer Experience.

ACTION ITEM

Pay attention to the details, not just the major elements, of your business.

Picture yourself in a gymnastics competition where, at the end of a performance, the judges hold up their individual score-cards—9.1, 9.4, 9.7. But it's the cumulative score that determines the final ranking of the gymnasts. It's the same for your company. You have to be concerned with a few big things, and hundreds of little things. It's the cumulative attention to detail that will ultimately win over your customers. Customers know they have options and choices, and if you don't manage your T-C-E, they just may go somewhere else.

WAY 104

When Do You Need It?

One of the secrets to meeting and exceeding your deadlines is
not to tell customers when you can do something for them, but
rather to ask them when they would like to have it. You have
to understand their timeframe. Often, their deadlines may not
be nearly as soon or as critical as you think. They may need
something in a week that you thought they would want in a day.
There are two main benefits that come from properly assessing
your customers' needs. The first is the opportunity to exceed
their expectations and get products and services to them more
quickly than needed. The second is to schedule your work and
your production to meet their needs, not yours.

ACTION ITEM

Work first to get your customer's ideal deadline. Then, if necessary, negotiate on the actual deadline with which you both can live.

While giving a guided tour of his Phoenix-based promotional-item company, Jim was explaining how deadlines have changed, and how much faster our lives move. Just a decade ago, he said, when an order came in for custom-printed items like business cards or coffee mugs, his company was excited if they could complete the order and ship it back to the customer in ten days. Today, these orders often come in with the first mail at 8:00 a.m., and are finished and headed out of the plant by 10:00 a.m. It's a fast-paced world.

Lost Sales = Opportunities

Lost sales, special orders, and buyouts can be opportunities to businesses that have the right inventories and are paying attention to what their customers want and need.

ACTION ITEM

Keep your inventory up-to-date and track all your orders. The goal is always to have what you should have and never to have what you shouldn't.

When one small store started keeping records of special purchases and items on which they lost sales, they quickly found one particular item they didn't stock that they had reordered five times for a customer. When the store offered to stock the item, the customer promised that it would get all his business. By tracking just one special purchase, this store ended up with a profitable new account. What are you doing to keep track of items you don't have? Do you analyze those special orders and lost sales?

WAY 106

Let Them Decide

There is no way to estimate your customers' willingness to spend money on the repairs, improvements, products, or services they really want. Never tell customers how they should invest their money. Let them make the decision. Don't throw cold water on a possible sale when you don't know the value of the item or transaction customers are considering. Sentimental value, emotions, and history often play into a customer's decision to spend more than you may think makes sense.

ACTION ITEM

Put your customers in the power position, give them their options, and then let them make the decision. Value is in the eye of the beholder.

The owner of a high-rise office building in downtown Chicago attempted to sell the building, which had fallen into disrepair and was vacant. When one prospect came in, he began to belittle the value of the building, talking about the leaky roof, the loose bricks, and other major problems. There was no way for the seller to know how much or how badly this prospect wanted to own the building. The more the prospect talked the property down, the more the seller lowered the price. Finally, they reached a deal. Then, unexpectedly, the new owner had the building demolished and the site cleared. He knew the value of the land, which was what he really wanted all along. The seller lost thousands of dollars because he assumed the buyer wanted the building, not the land.

TAKEAWAY

Your job is to inform prospects of their options; their job is to decide what best fits them and their budgets, needs, and wants.

Forget Satisfied

In years past, the goal of businesses was to satisfy their customers. Everyone thought that "satisfaction" was the key word. Satisfaction was a sure-fire way to foster relationships, encourage customer loyalty, and build repeat business. Now we know that it's not enough. Businesses must raise the bar and strive to go from good to great. They have to *delight*, not satisfy, their customers.

ACTION ITEM

Make a sign for your office/service area with the single word "Satisfied" on it. Then cross it out and write the word "Delighted" above it to remind everyone that this is the new standard. Delighted customers come from service as much as product.

The University of Michigan monitors customer satisfaction and rates business successes as it relates to customer satisfaction. Some researchers credit more demanding and better-informed customers as the driving force behind the move from "satisfied" to "delighted." What does this mean for you? You have to rethink, rework, and realign your goals, systems, procedures, and training. You have to find the strategies and tactics that yield an outcome of delighted customers, and adjust your practices accordingly.

WAY 108

Perceptions of Value

In prospecting today, we often throw around terminology that is not supported by facts and figures. "Unique selling position," "economies of scale," "service philosophy," and "brand promise" are all examples of words that require more information before they can be used effectively. It's amazing how most companies assume, and make poorly informed judgments about, how their prospects and customers perceive the value of goods and services.

Don't operate in the dark. Conduct surveys to get a true grasp of how your customers view you and perceive the value you are providing. Then communicate that value to your prospects so they can become loyal customers, too!

At Tuckman Cleaners, a sign hangs from the ceiling of each location that says: "The only opinion of value that counts is our customers' perception of value."

TAKEAWAY

Regardless of the words, terms, and phrases you use, at the end of the day, customers buy value.

WAY 109

Leverage Hulk and Bulk

Don't overlook the power of hulk and bulk to send a message to your prospects that you are an expert, you are serious, and you can be trusted to have what they want. Large displays and huge stacks of inventory help establish a visual memory that connects your company with a specific item so that customers will think of you when they need the product in the future.

ACTION ITEM

When you advertise, show lots of your product. Put it by the doors, in the aisles, or at the checkout counter. Focus on two or three items that will attract customers, and overwhelm them with quantity.

Greg runs a farm equipment dealership whose primary product line is John Deere. Driving by Greg's store in season is an experience. People see riding mowers and lawn equipment in huge stacks higher than the building. Out front, they see dozens of tractors, trailers, front-loaders, and other heavy equipment lined up ready for delivery. His displays, which use hulk and bulk to impress, are one of the key reasons why Greg's store is one of the largest in the region.

TAKEAWAY

Hulk and bulk establishes a visual memory that connects your company with a specific item so customers will think of you when they need that product.

It's All about Value

If you want to get your coworkers to see the value of your prospects, talk to them in terms of a their annual spending and how much they could be worth over a lifetime. It gives your employees and staff an entirely new perspective on prospective customers.

ACTION ITEM

Teach your associates the value of long-term customers, then encourage them to delight your long-term customers by doing extra little things to show them appreciation. Enhance the value of your business by adding extra benefits.

One executive found that his average member contributed $550 in gross profit to his association each year, and that the average member stayed on the roster a total of six and a half years. That adds up to $3,575 per member! The association quickly learned that they could really invest in recruitment, because they would make it up in the long-term.

WAY 111

How Much Does It Cost?

Customers want to know what they're getting into before making a purchase. So give them all the pricing information they need to make a decision. Items without prices may appear valueless to your customers and many people are too timid or feel they will be obligated to buy if they ask for a price.

ACTION ITEM

Do a daily sweep of your facility to make sure everything has a price so customers won't see your products as valueless.

One retailer who had a 300-piece tool display noticed that customers spun the rack, picked items up and looked them over, but then put them back and walked out the door. He suspected the problem was that there weren't prices on the items, and that people were too timid, too busy, or just not interested enough to ask. So he tried an experiment. He put price tags on all 300 items. Instantly, sales increased by 40 percent. Could simply having prices on his merchandise really increase sales that much?

There was only one way to find out. The retailer went back and carefully removed all 300 price stickers and tracked sales for the next sixty days. Amazingly, sales went right back to their previous level. He proved that everything has to be priced, or customers will see it as valueless and simply walk away.

TAKEAWAY

Customers will not ask for a price because they expect it to be there. If it's not, you are violating their expectations, and they'll probably take a hike.

WAY 112

Stack Up the Benefits

When you talk about the features of your product or service, be sure to explain its benefits. Here are three good phrases you can use:

1. "What that means to you is . . ."
2. "That is important to know because . . ."
3. "You will love this, because it will help you . . ."

ACTION ITEM

Become great at communicating both features and benefits, and your prospects will see that you are really selling value. This will make them want to become your customer.

When you buy a drill, what are you really purchasing? The drill? The bit? Nope. You want to be able to take that drill and make a hole. Being able to make a hole is the benefit of the tool, and is really what you are purchasing from the hardware store. It is very easy to get so caught up in talking about the features of your products that you overlook their real benefits. And at the end of the day, customers want to buy benefits.

> **TAKEAWAY**
>
> *At the end of the day, people don't buy what products are, they buy what products will do.*

What You Can Do

It is so easy to see the negatives in life and completely miss the positives. It's easy to see the ruts in the road instead of the beautiful highway. As you hunt for new customers, you will doubtless find competitors who are bigger, better, and more established who will present a real challenge for you. The secret is to focus on what you *can* do, without overlooking what you *can't* do.

ACTION ITEM

Keep yourself and your sales team focused on the positive. Then show your associates your own positive attitude. Always have three positive things to say to your team.

Herb worked in a small company that had three sales representatives. He was the author of doom and gloom. If the company asked him to work a special price promotion, you can bet he said the price was too high. If they took on a new product line, he whined and complained that it was the wrong brand. Herb dragged the other people in the company down so much that management decided to invite him to work somewhere else. Are you focused on the positives or the negatives in your attempts to get new customers?

WAY 114

Sell Value, Not Price

When you pick up a Sunday newspaper, you see lots of flyers and inserts promoting low prices. When you walk through a mall, you see signs for sales, promotions, and great deals. Most merchants make price their key selling issue. But when you cave in to pricing pressures, you may be giving money away. While price is important, it is never at the top of the list for most buyers. Stand your ground and sell value. It may have a bigger payoff than lowering your price.

ACTION ITEM

Have all your employees write out why you are justified in your pricing, features, benefits, and guarantees on all your major products or services.

There are only two types of buyers in the world: price-based buyers who try to get the best deal on every purchase, and value-based buyers who want to know what they're going to get for their money. If both of these buyers are smart, they will ask you about price. The price-based buyer is testing you to see if you will come down; the value-based buyer is testing you to see if you really believe in your price and product.

If you sell on value, when people ask about price, just give them the amount, and then say: "And I'm as surprised as you are that we can afford to sell for that. May I explain to you why you'd be smart to invest your money in this?" This can help you overcome the price barrier. But the main thing is for you to stand firm and believe that what you're selling is worth what you're asking. If you don't believe in your product, you will never convince your buyers to.

TAKEAWAY

The easiest selling method in the world is to cave in and lower the price, which means you are giving away money. Are you sure that's what you want to do?

The $10 Stupidity

Have you noticed how many businesses run expensive ads, offer deep discounts, tempt you with coupons and giveaways, and come up with all kinds of enticements to get you to buy? Then, when it comes time to take your money, they can't do it. They have lines backed up, salespeople who aren't properly trained, or counter people who have no customer-service experience. An additional person or a little more training could fix this problem, and make a bad experience a pleasurable one for as little as ten dollars an hour.

ACTION ITEM

Analyze your procedures and make it easy for your customers to buy. Human beings are creatures of habit who will always take the path of least resistance.

When it comes time to get customers to say "yes," don't be guilty of a $10 stupidity. Hire that extra staff, train your current associates, or invest in that extra piece of machinery that will make working under pressure much simpler. Work to make it easy, enjoyable, and quick for your customers to buy. Because if you are not ready when the customer is finally willing to hand over the cash, you're in big trouble.

If you make it a goal to have the right people with the right training and the right attitude in the right place at the right time, you'll turn prospects into buying customers more than ever before.

Losing Their Luster

Coupons, discounts, and promotions are so overused today that they are no longer an effective motivator to get new customers and boost sales. For example, almost every supermarket has overpriced their merchandise. To get it reduced to the price you should pay, you have to carry one of their frequent-buyer cards. Consider a different approach by using premiums, gifts, and other incentives to get customers to do business with you.

ACTION ITEM

Get in touch with a premium supplier who can fix you up with different logo items, and try handing them out as gifts and incentives.

When one of my friends bought a painfully overpriced luxury SUV, he nearly got into a fight with a sales manager who refused to give him the free cap and jacket that his golfing buddies had gotten when they bought the same car. Don't lose sight of the fact that some of the most unique incentives have spurred people to switch suppliers and become customers when coupons and discounts probably had little meaning to them. Begin today to experiment with what motivates your customers to go the extra mile.

> **TAKEAWAY**
>
> *People make emotional decisions about what they buy and where they buy, but they like to justify their purchases with logical explanations.*

WAY 117

Tell Them What You Can Do

No driver likes to end up on a dead-end street, and no businessperson enjoys being left in a bad situation by a supplier. Develop a reputation for caring, trying, and helping. Anytime you have to tell customers what you *can't* do, also tell them what you *can* do. Always have the information available to offer your customers an alternative if you are not able to meet their needs. Make sure that there are no dead-ends if they deal with you.

ACTION ITEM

Identify the top ten times when you have been forced to say "no." Develop a few potential positive responses that can be partnered with the negative ones. For example, when you have to tell prospects that you can't get their order in time, be sure to say that you can give them a 20 percent discount.

In the well-known movie *Miracle on 34th Street*, Santa Claus made this principle work for Macy's during the busy Christmas shopping season. When a child sat on his lap and asked for a toy the store didn't have, he directed the child's parents to a competitor in the area. The parents were so amazed by Santa's behavior that they came back to Macy's and brought all their friends and family as well.

> **TAKEAWAY**
>
> *Anyone can say "no," "sorry," or "tough luck." You earn the respect and business of potential customers when you help them by telling them what you* **can** *do. Balance the negative with the positive, and be sure to give your customers options.*

Are You Listening?

Walter, a veteran sales rep, had a legendary reputation for talking and a costly reputation for not listening. On one sales call alone, a manufacturer's rep working with him picked up on three clear buying signals from the prospect, while Walter never even slowed down. He kept talking, even though the customer had heard everything he needed to hear. Because Walter didn't take the time to listen to his customer, he left without making the sale.

ACTION ITEM

Talk only one third of the time you are with prospects. If they don't talk, ask questions. Train yourself and your team to listen. After all, it's your customers' needs, not yours, that must be satisfied. Give them a chance to express their needs.

Great companies develop great people who know how to listen effectively. The problem is that most prospecting conversations aren't about talking and listening; they are about two people just waiting for the other to stop talking. Most prospects will drop buying signals when they're ready to close the deal. It's your job to make sure you can hear them!

WAY 119

The Early Bird Gets
the New Customer

Staying on the cutting edge of changes, new products and services, and new technologies is a must if you want to be perceived as the best resource for prospects and customers. It takes real work and a commitment from everyone to keep up with all the changes in our world today.

ACTION ITEM

Make it a point to be the most informed and up-to-date in your industry. Provide your staff with the tools they need and insist they use them. Make your associates the people with the latest information and your customers and prospects will learn that you can be depended on to be on the cutting edge.

Tom operates a group of successful retail stores spread across Iowa and Wisconsin. He believes one of their marketing advantages comes from making a major effort to monitor the industry for new information and changes that are happening in their marketplace. To keep up, he and his crew receive a variety of trade publications each month. They frequently walk the aisles of trade shows and manufacturers' exhibits, and they carefully monitor manufacturers' mailings to see what's new. They also invest in several newsletters, including a daily fax bulletin that keeps them informed of what is going on in their market. Tom's salespeople frequently know about changes and innovations days, weeks, and sometimes even months in advance—long before their competition even gets wind of what is going on. They are perceived by customers as the best resource for the information and products they need.

TAKEAWAY

Our world is changing by the second. If you don't change with it, you'll be listed in the "Who's Through" in your business category.

The Problem with Communication

In prospecting for new customers, effective communication can be incredibly challenging. So much of what we do is verbal that sometimes we forget that other kinds of communication can be just as effective. Don't forget that visual and written communication can play a big part in prospecting for new customers and keeping old ones.

ACTION ITEM

Create a backup system using email, voice mail, or written orders to make sure that no verbal orders are misunderstood—especially when they are orders from customers or requests for information from prospects!

Herb was a white-haired manager who called that white hair his "frost of wisdom." One of his favorite pieces of wisdom was just how dangerous verbal orders can be. He claimed that communication problems normally came from one of three situations:

1. No communication took place in the first place.

2. The original communication was misspoken or misunderstood.
3. Parties assumed they had answers and went ahead without confirming the information.

Herb had a bright-yellow form that he insisted everyone use that said "Avoid Verbal Orders" in big, bold letters across the top, and "Put It in Writing" along the bottom. What are you doing to make sure you communicate effectively within your organization and with your prospects?

TAKEAWAY

Remember that the message is always in the mind of the receiver. By putting it in writing, you vastly increase the likelihood that a message will be communicated correctly.

WAY 121

"No" Is Not the Answer

Fear is the greatest single challenge that you must overcome if you're going to be successful at turning prospects into customers.

When many salespeople hear the word "no," they give up or give in. But if you are going to succeed in prospecting for customers, you can't quit when you hear the word "no." You've got to step back, look at the situation, and try to find a new approach that will get your prospects to say "yes."

ACTION ITEM

Don't quit when you hear the word "no." Take a step back and think about what you tried. Then try something different. Keep going until you can change a "no" into a "yes."

Ron was a bright, young salesperson for a company in Chicago. He was organized, well-groomed, and articulate, and he kept great records about his sales prospecting. The only problem was that he wasn't getting new business, and no one in his company could figure out why. Finally, they hired a sales consultant to travel with Ron and critique his selling style. What they found was that, when a customer said "no," Ron quit and simply gave up. He was giving in and giving up instead of finding ways to overcome the "no" and change it to a "yes." Winston Churchill said: "It is not enough that we do our best. Sometimes we have to do what's required."

TAKEAWAY

You're not defeated until you give up. The moment you say "I quit," you have defeated yourself.

Selective Hearing

Beware of making promises, claims, or even casual comments. Customers have selective hearing and selective memory, and you can bet that they will remember conversations and interactions in a way that suits them best! If you tell customers you can get something in a week, they'll be calling you in three days wanting to know where it is. If you tell them you think you can get it for free, they'll want to know how much you're going to pay them to take it. And if you say you can do something and then have to renege, your chances of getting that customer to come back to you are very slim.

ACTION ITEM

When you make statements or promises that could be interpreted by prospects or customers as certain, remind them: "If it ain't in writing, it ain't so." Then, when you know you can make a promise, put it in writing for them.

When Betty, a financial-services representative, called on a potential customer, she told the person she was pretty certain that she could offer a promotional package at little or no cost. Those words came back to haunt her. On her very next prospecting call, the broker wanted to know where the "free complete promotional package" she had promised was. What she quickly learned was that a casual comment can be turned to a disadvantage.

WAY 123

If Only We Had Time

My grandfather used to say that both meetings and sermons should end on the same day they begin. He was a nut about wasting time. He recognized that there are only twenty-four hours in a day, so it's important to spend those hours wisely. It's vital to recognize the value of your customers' time, especially when they are investing that time in listening to you. The pressure on businesspeople today to get more done in less time is the biggest complaint that business owners and associates have.

ACTION ITEM

Make managing your time a critical ingredient of your prospecting, and let customers know what your expectations are up front.

Michael, an award-winning sales rep, follows the Vince Lombardi rule. If he's not ten minutes early for an appointment, he feels as if he is late. He believes a great deal of his success as a salesman is grounded in his respect for his customers' time. His three simple rules are:

1. Always be on time or early for your commitments.
2. Always be prepared—no fumbling, excuses, or stories.
3. Always end at the time you promised, and remind customers or prospects how much you value their time.

Are you always early, prepared, and respectful of other people's time? If not, it may be a real stumbling block to getting the new customers you want.

> **TAKEAWAY**
>
> *The phrase "time-management" is really a misnomer. You can't manage your time; you can only manage your life to fit into the time you have. Ultimately, if you respect your prospects' time, they will respect you.*

Anticipate Obstacles

Author John Newborn said: "People can be divided into three groups: those who make things happen, those who watch things happen, and those who wonder what happened." This certainly applies to people in business, particularly on the subject of gaining and retaining customers. The secret to success is to ask yourself which group you're in. An even better question to ask yourself is which group you *should* be in.

ACTION ITEM

Become a goal-oriented manager, especially when it comes to getting new customers.

Prominent author and business leader Frank Basile says that, when he teaches goal-setting, he teaches people to be goal-oriented. An important ingredient of his goal-setting training is to anticipate that there will be obstacles ahead that will have to be handled to reach those goals. He says to take the word "try" out of your vocabulary, because it sets you up for failure and excuses. Would you want to fly with a pilot who said he would "try" to land safely? When you set a goal, say to yourself: "I'm going to make this happen." Then get it done.

WAY 125

Decide Not to Sell

Many amateur salespeople think every sales call must be an attempt to make a sale. Experienced professionals know that there is often a great deal of research, investigation, and diagnosis necessary before they can possibly think about closing a deal.

ACTION ITEM

Probe, look, and listen. Be patient. Find your competitive advantages before trying to make the sale.

The owner of a service company was really nice to the salesperson each time she stopped by. However, he claimed he was getting the best price, the best delivery, and the best inventory management when he bought from someone else. It took her more than six months to learn that most of what he claimed wasn't true. In fact, many of his suppliers were taking advantage of him, and he wasn't paying enough attention. He had items that should have been returned; he had merchandise left over for which he would never get his money back; he had warranties that should have been credited long ago. After six months, this savvy salesperson finally made her case. When she presented it to the owner and clearly demonstrated that her total service package was better, he immediately went from the prospect column to the customer column.

TAKEAWAY

Remember that the goal of a sales call may not be to sell at all, but simply to gather critical information.

Bullet-Proof Your Communications

One of the most dangerous things you can do in prospecting for customers is to assume that true communication took place. We get so many magazines, letters, emails, and direct mailings, and so much personal mail, that it's easy for important details to slip through the cracks. You can bullet-proof your communications by having another set of eyes test what you are doing.

ACTION ITEM

Always check critical items going out to prospects by having a second set of eyes review the materials. Develop a system so that every item that goes out the door is double-checked for consistency and clarity. This type of proofing can catch a problem before it begins.

Elaine is an office assistant in a busy secretarial group. She has an uncanny ability to read and review materials to see if all the necessary details are there and to identify any communication gaps. In her office, they call it the "Elaine test." With any new creative piece—flyers, invitations, ads, and particularly events where people are invited and need to know a great deal of detail—the rule is "Give it to Elaine." If, after reading it, she can tell you the details about what is happening, then it's clear and concise. If Elaine can't relate the details about what is on the agenda, it is a clear indicator that the piece needs to be revised.

TAKEAWAY

Find someone in your office or group who can function like Elaine.

Attention to Detail

One thing prospects quickly notice and grow to admire is a representative who dots the "i's" and crosses the "t's." When you pay attention to both the big things and the little details, they quickly come to see that you are a person on whom they can depend. Don't ever let the big picture overwhelm your vision of success.

ACTION ITEM

Make yourself a card that says: "Who? What? When? Where? Why? and How much?" Pull it out anytime you want to test something to see if it is clear and complete.

The United States military is one of the most reliable organizations in the world. They run tests on anything and everything they do. Before running missions or engaging in any activity, they always try to answer the following questions: Who? What? When? Where? Why? and How much? These six questions give them a fairly complete idea of the task at hand. You can use them to provide the pertinent information you need when dealing with your prospects. Ask them before you start any project or assignment. Remember, you will never fail by giving too much attention to detail.

WAY 128

Use Your Design

Really successful prospectors maintain a constantly updated list of great ideas to improve their prospecting efforts. One key question you should always ask yourself is: "How can I multiply my prospecting efforts without investing in more manpower?" One answer is to work on the visibility of your vehicles to maintain top-of-mind awareness with your prospects.

ACTION ITEM

Investigate graphic design options and consider an entirely new way to identify your vehicles. Your goal is to catch people's attention and tell them who you are, what you do, and how to contact you.

Even small and mid-sized businesses with little or no budget can benefit from carving out a unique image for their vehicles, whether they have one or 100. Think about how quickly you recognize a black-and-white police car, an emergency vehicle, or a simple but effective yellow cab. If you have a bigger budget, consider how UPS has turned thousands and thousands of ugly brown trucks into an internationally known logo. All these icons have been developed as a result of intent, purpose, and design. Look at your company and identify unique factors you can exploit to enhance your visibility.

TAKEAWAY

Steal, don't invent, your success. When you see what successful people do and do something similar, you too become successful.

WAY 129

Smile, Smile, Smile

There are only two kinds of people when it comes to winning the hearts of new customers: those who should work for you and those who should never work for you. The difference between the two is sometimes hard to identify, but I'll give you a hint. It's all about smiles!

ACTION ITEM

Develop your own smile test. Let people try the job, and watch their facial expressions. It will tell you everything you need to know about the person's future with your company.

Across Japan, fast-food menus look just like those here in the United States: hamburgers, fries, and soft drinks. The one major difference is that, in the lower right-hand corner, they almost always say: "Smiles are Zero Yen." The bright attitude and good customer-service skills are free of charge, and are usually the reason customers return to a specific restaurant. When you hire new employees, make it a goal to hire only those applicants who have a big smile.

> **TAKEAWAY**
>
> *Even the grumpiest prospect wants to deal with someone who smiles. Make sure that person is from your organization.*

It's Okay to Know You Don't Know

Call it ego, pride, or vanity, but, however you label it, Americans are hesitant to admit when they don't know something. Really smart people know it is okay not to know, and spend their time and effort on finding the answer. Train your employees to ask for information if they don't know the answer, rather than lie or dismiss a customer request.

ACTION ITEM

When you know you don't know, admit it, and find someone who does. That should be a company policy. Otherwise, you drive away potential customers.

Raymond drove nearly fifty miles to a computer store because he needed a highly technical part. When he asked whether the item would really do the job, the sales clerk responded: "I think so." That immediately set off Raymond's built-in lie detector. He exited the store and headed to a competitor, where he found a reliable answer to his question. Raymond believed it was okay for someone not to know the answer, as long as that person was willing to get someone who did.

WAY 131

Don't Be a Bungling Bob

Dale Carnegie taught that selling is about relationships—15 percent is about *what* you know; 85 percent is about *who* you know. While that principle is simple, it can also be problematic. If you don't know the 15 percent about your products and services, it can ruin your credibility with prospects and sabotage your customer service.

ACTION ITEM

Make it a rule each month to read your primary sales materials, bulletins, and promotions so you know in advance how to answer your prospects' questions. Also, be sure to provide the materials to your prospects directly.

Each month, Bob's warehouse produced a list of their specials for the month and, each month, Bob's customers asked him about those specials. But when they did, Bob had to go out to his car and search through piles of paper to find the monthly flyers. When he brought them in, rumpled and covered with coffee stains, he proceeded to read them to his prospects. Finally, one of his prospects said: "Bob, I've given you a nickname—Bungling Bob—because you don't seem to care enough to learn about your own products and services. You also insult me, because I can read those materials myself." Bob got a huge dose of the truth that day, and has since tried to treat his customers with dignity and respect. He makes sure that his materials are neat and organized, and he now has his special flyers mailed directly to his customers.

TAKEAWAY

When your prospects find out that you don't know, they think you don't really care about them, and they won't deal with you.

Create Your Personal Gold Mine

Do you know what is more worthless than yesterday's newspaper, week-old bread, or a five-year-old phonebook? It's a database that isn't accurate. Your future success in winning over new customers will be determined largely by the quality and size of your prospect list. Today is the best opportunity you will ever have to make a commitment to keep that list up to date, accurate, and on target.

ACTION ITEM

Create a form that everyone can use to notify you when changes occur in your prospect list, and have them keep it by their phones or desks so they can use it easily.

Early on, Joanne realized how powerful a well-maintained, up-to-date list of prospects can be. She made a commitment to do several things to keep her database accurate.

1. Pick up the telephone and verify the information anytime she was notified of a change by people in her company.

2. Alert coworkers to pass along any information they got about changes in a prospect's situation, including people, phone numbers, or addresses.

3. Add the term "Address Correction Requested" below the return address on all company mailings so the post office would alert her to changes.

If you're going to keep your database accurate, it is essential to have a multi-strategic approach to gaining and maintaining good information.

TAKEAWAY

If you invest in taking care of your future-customer database, your future-customer database will take care of you.

WAY 133

The Insanity Principle

Albert Einstein formulated something that he called the "insanity principle," which claims that sane people cannot continue to do the same thing many times over and expect to get a different outcome.

ACTION ITEM

Always ask yourself what you could have done differently
and what you could have said differently each time you
make a cold call. Create a diary of your responses and
study them to find different approaches based on your
own observations.

In one year, a sales professional made over 600 cold calls on
600 different businesses. With each call, he slowly but surely con-
quered his fear of the unknown. After every cold call, he asked
himself two questions: What should I have *done* differently? and
What should I have *said* differently? Then he reread his answers
for his ten most recent calls and used that information to tweak
subsequent customer calls and make them just a little different
to ensure a better reception.

> **TAKEAWAY**
>
> *Learn completely from every experience and use
> that learning to improve subsequent customer calls.*

Beware of Fatal Ruts

Do you know the difference between a rut and a grave? A rut is a grave with the ends knocked out. It is easy to fall into a rut and take customers for granted. When this happens, your presentations will come off as parrot-like, simply repeating things again and again.

ACTION ITEM

Prepare every presentation as if it were the first time you've done it. Sometimes it's just a matter of putting on your game face. Prospects and customers can tell when they are not getting your best effort.

Each time you give a presentation to a prospective customer, pretend you are doing it for the very first time. Get involved, watch the key points, ask the right questions, and walk your prospects through it. Remember, they are seeing it with fresh eyes. Don't come off like a parrot.

If your presentation doesn't send a message that you care, your prospect will get a message that you don't care.

WAY 135

Ask for Help

Something magical happens when you call on customers accompanied by a specialist. It's interesting how prospects who previously wouldn't give you the time of day will suddenly stop and listen to a person they see as an authority. Don't be afraid to reach out and get help from manufacturers, distributors, and retailers who can help you win over prospects.

ACTION ITEM

Make a list of all the people who may be able to help you, then ask for their help and make some calls. You'll be surprised how supportive your allies will be and how effective you'll become.

Examine your marketplace and ask yourself who can help you. Then, when help is available, knock on the doors of those prospects who may not have given you the time of day in the past. Introduce your specialists and see what happens. There's something about having that second person traveling with you that seems to open locked doors. It may be uncomfortable or awkward, but it's always productive. Don't be afraid to ask for help.

WAY 136

Accentuate the Positive

A positive attitude can be the #1 ingredient in your ability to get new customers. As the saying goes: "Any fool can criticize, condemn, and complain, and most of them do." Your success in business means that you will not be allowed to pick the people with whom you work, so just make up your mind to make the most of it. It's not who you encounter that will determine your success; it's how you respond to the people you encounter that will make the difference.

ACTION ITEM

Each day, pick three positive things you can talk about. If it's raining, point out how that can help corn grow. If it's cold, point out how that will create jobs, because people may need to buy coats. If the wind's blowing, talk about how that will generate power at the new windmills around the country.

Experienced professionals identify three things you can do when you encounter people who criticize, condemn, or complain:

1. Beware and monitor your own words. Don't get caught up in their negativity. This can create a downward spiral that can destroy both of you.

2. Don't chime in and comment on their negatives, because you will only perpetuate them. Often, these people are just testing you.

3. When appropriate, change the subject to something positive. Get them in an upbeat mood, and everyone will be happier.

WAY 137

Harness the Internet

There's no better resource than the Internet to keep you up to date on research, facts and figures, what competitors are doing, and what's on the horizon for your business. By harnessing the Internet's power, you can prepare to win customers to your business.

ACTION ITEM

Teach everyone to use the Internet, and make doing research a must when trying to turn prospects into customers.

You can find anything on the web, from how to raise fishing worms to a protocol for flying the American flag. Statistics on the population in your area, as well as records of births and deaths, are instantly available online. If you're not using these tools, you're not resolving the ignorance problem. You can out-smart and outpace your competition by using the Internet as your research vehicle

WAY 138

Tell the Truth

Most businesspeople know the difference between right and wrong, and they know the difference between honesty and deception. But there are still people who operate in shades of gray and convince themselves that it is okay to deceive, manipulate, and play with the truth to get new customers. A practice of telling the truth, the whole truth, and nothing but the truth will work for you in the long term.

Use this as an advertising test: Is this true, and will people believe it?

Think of the gold company whose ad claims: "Analysts predict the price of gold could double in the future." While that prediction is not illegal (although it probably should be), it sure smacks of an attempt to convince you that gold is a sure thing, and that buying from them will give you a great return and riches untold. But it's deceptive. Yes, gold *could* double in the future, but who knows when, and who will guarantee it?

TAKEAWAY

You will never get in trouble trying to attract customers by telling the truth, the whole truth, and nothing but the truth.

How Are You Really Doing?

One sure test of your ability to attract more customers is to ask how you are doing with the customers you already have. Most businesses rarely ask that question, thinking that a lack of complaints means everyone is happy. The reality is that you will only hear from two types of customers: those who love you and those who are unhappy with you. The killer is the great silent majority who don't whine or complain. They just quietly leave you for your competitors.

ACTION ITEM

Create a system that regularly invites customers to sound off so you know how your services rate. This will help you attract and retain the prospects you want.

When a salesman asked how his company was doing at making deliveries to Bob's mechanical repair department, he was flabbergasted to learn that Bob thought their service needed some work. Bob said that, in recent months, the service had deteriorated and that he had had to go to a nearby competitor when he needed something in a hurry. The salesman was smart enough to spend the remainder of the day polling his other customers in the area. He found that their service had deteriorated so badly that many customers were abandoning them.

A late-afternoon meeting with his key people determined that they had taken on some businesses in outlying areas and that it was keeping their people and trucks tied up so they couldn't deliver to their existing good customers. The end result was that they had to tell some outlying customers they were sorry they couldn't serve them, and rebuild their service for the customers who were their mainstay. How are you doing with your service? What would your customers really say if an outsider polled them at this very moment?

TAKEAWAY

A lack of complaints doesn't mean your customers are out of ammunition. It may simply mean they are reloading, and they're going to come after you again.

WAY 140

Meet Uncle F-E-S-S

You already know that getting new customers takes persistence, hard work, and lots of homework. If you don't anticipate objections, roadblocks, or excuses (and have answers for them), then you're going to be lonelier than the Maytag repairman. The secret is to know in advance what you're going to say and do when a customer presents an objection.

ACTION ITEM

Identify and work on scripting answers to your top 10 F-E-S-S (Frequently Encountered Sales Situations). Know in advance how you're going to respond to customers' questions.

Joe was a real pro at selling training programs and earned a six-figure income because he had answers to objections before they came along. He called these his Uncle F-E-S-S, or Frequently Encountered Sales Situations. He anticipated what buyers might say and was ready to deal with it in advance. For example, when one prospect said he wasn't going to buy Joe's training program because some of his people weren't going to use it, Joe complimented him and told him he was absolutely correct. However, Joe also said that research had proven that some of his salespeople *would* embrace the training program, would have huge sales increases, and would make him a lot of money. He was right. The gentleman signed the purchase order for the training materials and Joe went to the bank, having turned a prospect into a new customer.

WAY 141

Don't Drop In

Prospects want and need to feel valued, respected, and accepted. And they will respond to your efforts to make them feel that way. Telling customers that you are calling on them because you "just happen to be in the area" tells them that you are an accidental tourist without planning or forethought. It destroys your credibility. Always make customers feel special because you came just to see them, regardless of how many other people you may see that day or what your plans are.

ACTION ITEM

Learn what makes prospects feel valued, respected, and accepted. Deliver that to them and watch your new-customer count soar.

When Bob, a seasoned insurance company representative, made calls on his prospects, he made them feel so valuable that they felt guilty if they didn't buy from him. Whether he saw only one prospect or ten in a given day, he had the ability to make them all feel as if they were the only company he visited. What can you do to let prospects know they are the most important people in the world, and that you're coming to see them because you value them?

WAY 142

Don't Love Them and Leave Them

His name was John Cash Penney, but you probably know him better by the retail store he founded—JCPenney. As a retailing pioneer, John Cash Penney believed the best service you could give was the service that came after the sale. He knew that following up with customers and backing up what you say and do is crucial, because it leads to long-term customer relationships.

ACTION ITEM

Look at the products and/or services you provide your customers. Which of them could be used to follow up with a customer as a means of building a relationship? Which are most likely to cause problems? Based on the answers to these questions, develop a "service after the sale" program to help you retain those valuable new customers.

John Deere, maker of everything from lawn tractors to combines, launched a new program to sell its expensive high-quality lawn tractors. With each purchase, the buyer was promised that, after he had used the lawn tractor a few times, a service technician from John Deere would come to run a six-point inspection. The service person would make absolutely certain the machine was in perfect working order and that everything was adjusted properly, so that the customer could be assured of many years of mowing with little maintenance. This gave John Deere the opportunity to catch a problem before it became a disaster. It was also a chance to remind customers that they had invested in a high-quality product that would probably save them a lot of money by avoiding emergency service incidents in the future. What can you do to offer your customers service after the sale so they will look to you for future purchases?

Providing service after the sale works great, because almost nobody does it.

WAY 143

Organize Your Prospects

If you need to organize, track, and cultivate numerous prospects, investing in software specifically designed for managing a database of potential customers may be a great investment for you. It can help you formalize, organize, and systemize your prospecting efforts and create reports to show how you are progressing.

ACTION ITEM

Research available database applications and select one that best fits your company. Then build a database of customers. Remember that any database is only valuable if it is kept up to date.

Many sales representatives who are drop-dead serious about cultivating new customers have been overwhelmed by the many things a database application can do for them. Check out popular brands like ACT, Goldmine, Microsoft Access, or Microsoft Outlook to understand how you can systemize your contacts. These automated software applications give you great opportunities to do mailings, keep sales-call records, send emails and faxes, and print custom letters to your prospects. If you're trying to manage a large number of prospects, a good database application is a must.

TAKEAWAY

The secret to developing new customers is to have a systemized approach for consistently going after prospects.

WAY 144

The Agony of Defeat

Let's face it. Sometimes the work and effort of prospecting and getting new customers is tough. You hear the word "no" again and again. You feel defeated, and everything inside you wants to quit and walk away. You want to give up and go home. The answer is not to give in to defeat. Instead, have a plan to rebuild your energy and spirit when you feel the battle is lost.

ACTION ITEM

Identify people you can call on who will encourage you. Make a plan so that, when you feel beat up and ready to quit, you've got somewhere to go, somewhere to renew your energy and spirit.

When Ed called on us, he was always an excited, wound-up, and ready-to-go salesman. Every one of our people enjoyed seeing him come in, and we worked hard to sell his products. One afternoon, I asked him if he ever felt down, discouraged, or defeated. When he acknowledged that he did, I was shocked. Then I asked him what he did when he was in that defeated mode. He told me that he called on the customers who liked him, supported him, believed in him, and encouraged him. When I asked who they were, he said: "One of them is you. When I feel defeated, I call on you and a couple of others, and you get me going again. It's my plan for overcoming that feeling of defeat."

> **TAKEAWAY**
>
> *The thrill of victory and the agony of defeat
> are human feelings. The secret lies not in what
> happens but in how you respond to it.*

Expect the Unexpected

When working to win new customers, you are certain to have set-backs, disappointments, and discouragements. The reality of trying to win new customers is that, at times, you will not succeed. There will be speed bumps and unexpected challenges. Your success in getting new customers is not about what happens to you, however. Your success will be forged by how you respond to what happens to you. You have to learn to expect the unexpected.

ACTION ITEM

Write out "Expect the Unexpected" and remember it when dealing with unusual circumstances.

When you've spent months working to win a new customer's business, you know the devastating feelings and emotions associated with hearing those fateful words "no," "sorry," or "we've gone with someone else." What can you do? You can either get better or get bitter. Everyone can make the choice to turn their stumbling blocks into stepping-stones by improving their competitive skills. Use setbacks as a reminder that "no thank you" can be a challenge to you and use those experiences as a force multiplier. You are a survivor, so pick up the pieces and go looking for new customers.

Great salespeople are those who have been knocked down 1,000 times—and gotten up 1,001 times.

WAY 146

You Can't Afford Not To

Perception is the most important word when you are trying to bring new customers into your business. Invest in your image, especially when you are attempting to convince customers that you should be their preferred choice. Business cards, envelopes, brochures, and all printed materials (more than any other single factor) can reflect your value more than the words you use.

ACTION ITEM

Make a connection with a graphic designer and/or printing facility that can print your materials in small quantities and store them.

Make a decision that you're not going to be an amateur, but that you're going to move up to the professional's level. In today's high-tech world of desktop publishing and instant printing, choose quality over quantity with everything that your customers may see.

WAY 147

Become an Information Junkie

In today's market, where information is everywhere, it is awfully easy to overlook it. One of the things you can do to endear yourself to prospects and customers is to become a source of information that interests them. Use your association memberships, trade journals, daily newspapers, and the mail as resources for information your customers may value. Never assume they already have the information. Because so much comes across their desks, there is probably no way they can keep up with it all.

A note and a copy of some strategic information can tell customers you are really sincere about helping them meet their needs.

ACTION ITEM

Use your association memberships, trade journals, and other resources to become an information junkie. Identify your top ten prospects and determine the various things you could send to them.

My friend Dick has an uncanny ability for finding things that interest me. From a postcard while he's traveling, to an article about one of my hobbies, to a prediction about the future, he always seems to stay one step ahead of me. Opening mail from him, or even getting an email, is always exciting, because I know it will contain something that is targeted just to me. Keep top-of-mind awareness and build an outpost in your prospects' minds where they see you as someone who is truly tuned in to their needs. In a world that doesn't care, you will be a breath of fresh air.

TAKEAWAY

There is no way to predict when that one item you send to prospects could be the one that opens the door to all of their business.

Obsessed with Reputation

The dictionary defines reputation as "the views that are generally held about somebody or something." In other words, when people think about doing business with you, your reputation is going to be a big part of whether they decide to go with you or with someone else. Very few business owners and managers realize the need for, the value in, and the role of reputation in gaining and retaining customers.

ACTION ITEM

Find out what your reputation or your company's reputation is in the marketplace by asking. Then assume that, if one person is unhappy, ten more are unhappy but haven't told you. Become someone who is obsessed with protecting and safeguarding your reputation.

Take a lesson from the Michelin Tire Company, which, over the years, has built a reputation for having the highest quality tires. When their fourteen cars (more than half the field) pulled out of the 2005 U. S. Grand Prix in Indianapolis, thousands of people were up in arms that they had been cheated. Almost immediately, Michelin protected their reputation by apologizing to the people who had bought tickets and spending a reported

$10 million to give refunds to those who felt they had gotten a raw deal. You can bet that was a painful event for Michelin, but, in years to come, they will recover all that money, because they did the right thing to protect their reputation.

WAY 149

Invest in Yourself

Do you take good care of your family, your spouse or significant other, and your parents? Do you support your community, civic organizations, and the important things that take place in your neighborhood? Good for you! You deserve a pat on the back. Now, how about taking care of yourself? Isn't it time you invested in your future and your success in dealing with people? Regardless of the product or service you sell, the reality is that you're in the people business, and you just happen to sell the product or service you're dealing with today.

ACTION ITEM

Check out the training providers in your area that offer programs on leadership, sales, interpersonal relationships, and a variety of other subjects. There are many good ones out there, including my favorite—the Dale Carnegie courses.

When Jimmy was nineteen years old, he had such a poor self-image that he hated to look at himself in the mirror. He hadn't done well in school, he was never good at sports, and he was always overweight. Then he saw an ad for an inspirational seminar that promised to help develop self-confidence, and he enrolled in a Dale Carnegie course. He was absolutely amazed that, in just a few weeks, his investment turned his life in a totally different direction. The Carnegie course gave him the tools he needed to feel good about himself, and to feel good about his ability to deal with other people. Isn't it time you invested in yourself? Most top salespeople are Dale Carnegie graduates. You should be, too.

TAKEAWAY

Author James Allen said: "A man is literally what he thinks." If you think better of yourself, you will be more successful.

The Value of Persistence

When you ask customers for their business once, it's very unlikely you'll get a significant percentage to say "yes." But as you continue to ask the second, third, and fourth time, the percentage increases dramatically. The fifth time you ask is almost magic. Perhaps that's because customers realize your persistence indicates the kind of service you will give them.

ACTION ITEM

Be persistent. Keep reminding your customers that you are there and available, and eventually they will bite. In the meantime, do all the things we have discussed that will keep you at the top of their minds for when the time is right.

One way to win new customers is to let them know that you will play second fiddle to their current supplier. By positioning yourself as the second choice, you have the opportunity to be there when their current supplier makes a blunder. The secret is to be in their faces at the point of need or when they want to make a change. That means being persistent. Keep asking, and eventually their suppliers will drop the ball and you will get the business. How do we know that? How many times have you dropped the ball?

> **TAKEAWAY**
> _____
>
> *The phrase "out of sight, out of mind" couldn't be more true. Be persistent to win new business.*

About the Author

Decades ago, when Jerry Wilson began his professional career managing one small auto parts store, it would have been hard to imagine that he would become a world-renowned expert in marketing who would develop an innovative marketing and customer-retention philosophy.

Yet that is just what happened. Jerry grew his small auto parts store into an extremely profitable retail group that dominated the area in which it was located. Not content with simply increasing sales in his own business, Jerry leveraged and expanded his experience, soon becoming well known for his retail operations and his sales-and-management consulting.

Jerry authored the highly acclaimed books, *Word-of-Mouth Marketing, 138 Quick Ideas to Get More Clients*, and *How to Grow Your Auto Parts Business*, published in numerous languages and distributed internationally. He also contributed more than 100 feature articles on customer retention to a variety of association and industry trade journals in both the United States and Canada.

As a result of his experiences, Jerry developed a new marketing philosophy called "Customerology" to aid companies in gaining and retaining satisfied customers. As a consultant, he assisted companies like Firestone, Merchants Tire, Stanley Publishing, and Ripley's Believe It or Not!, helping them rethink customer retention, service strategies, and business practices. He also served as executive director for a large state trade association and consulted with both national and international business leaders.

In New Zealand, Jerry worked hand in hand with management to overhaul Rainbow's End Theme Park after its rescue from bankruptcy. After revamping its customer-relations system in accordance with Jerry's advice, the theme park realized a 70,000-attendee increase over the previous year—quantifiable success as a result of the tenets of Customerology.

At Merchant's Tire, a 100-plus chain of tire and auto-service stores based in Virginia, Jerry assisted management with a campaign to reduce customer complaints. After implementing the Customerology system, the chain saw customer complaints plummet by more than half.

These astounding successes led to numerous speaking engagements. As a professional speaker, Jerry appeared before more than 1,000 groups and traveled to all fifty states, as well as Canada, New Zealand, Indonesia, and South America. His keynote presentations, seminars, and workshops benefited countless companies and organizations worldwide.

Jerry was awarded the Certified Speaking Professional (CSP) designation by the National Speakers Association (NSA), a prestigious award given to only 400 speakers worldwide. He served two terms as president of the Indiana chapter of the NSA and also served as chair of the its CSP certification committee.

Jerry was honored by being listed in the Who's Who Directory of the Midwest and in the World Directory of Men of Achievement.